Success at a Price

Success at a Price

Women of Color Students at a White University

Lisa C. Huebner,

Samantha Jeune,

and Odette Kolenky

University of Georgia
ATHENS

Sociology of Race and
Ethnicity web page

Set in 10.5/13.5 Garamond Premier Pro Regular
by Rebecca A. Norton

Most University of Georgia Press titles are
available from popular e-book vendors.

Printed digitally

Library of Congress Cataloging-in-Publication Data

Names: Huebner, Lisa C. author | Jeune, Samantha
    author | Kolenky, Odette author
Title: Success at a price : women of color students at a white university
    / Lisa C. Huebner, Samantha Jeune, and Odette Kolenky.
Description: Athens, Georgia : University of Georgia Press, [2025] |
    Series: Sociology of race and ethnicity | Includes bibliographical
    references and index. | Contents: Diversity dilemmas: whose
    success and at what cost? — "You are welcome here": failed
    promises — "I want to say something": the price of bridging
    labor — "What are you?": the daily normal — "Assume whatever
    you want about me, but let me blow your mind": successes and
    strategies — Diversity solutions: redefining student success.
Identifiers: LCCN 2024052566 (print) | LCCN 2024052567 (ebook) |
    ISBN 9780820373607 hardback | ISBN 9780820373614 paperback |
    ISBN 9780820373621 epub | ISBN 9780820373638 pdf
Subjects: LCSH: Minority women in higher education—
    Social conditions | Women, Black—Education (Higher) |
    Academic achievement | Racism in higher education | Educational
    equalization | Universities and colleges—Social aspects
Classification: LCC LC1567 .H74 2025 (print) | LCC LC1567 (ebook) |
    DDC 378.1/9822089—dc23/eng/20250222
LC record available at https://lccn.loc.gov/2024052566
LC ebook record available at https://lccn.loc.gov/2024052567

CONTENTS

ACKNOWLEDGMENTS

Lisa: To begin, I sincerely thank all the women of color students—past, present, and future—whom I have had the pleasure of teaching, who have taught me, and who have influenced me in countless ways. I thank you for your courage and for your wisdom. I thank you for your time, energy, and stories. I thank you for motivating this book. This book is for you.

I thank our research participants and our research team: C. E. Brown, Sam Jeune, Odette Kolenky, and Christa Rivers, who are all amazing and brilliant in their own rights. I am so grateful to them for trusting me and for sharing their intellectual and creative insights with me, with one another, with our participants, and with many academic communities throughout the duration of this project. I learned so much from each of them. On behalf of the team, I would also like to thank Irissa Baxter-Luper and Yami Reyes, who helped us research and organize our literature as graduate students at the time.

I especially thank Sam and Odette for agreeing to write this book with me. I mean, in my mind, it was the only way, but given how much they both have going in their exceptionally wonderful and beautiful lives, the opportunity to write with them was truly a gift to me and to the project overall. I am eternally grateful for their insight and their thoughtfulness as well as their tenacity in seeing this through. This book—like the project from the start—is so much better because of them. Thank you, Sam, and thank you, Odette, so very much. As Odette said, we did it!

I thank my friends and colleagues who helped to create and administer the first mentorship program as described in this book, let me ramble on, helped me think through everything, read my writing, and championed this work in countless ways over many years' time: Dr. Sendy Alcidonis, Dr. Jen Bacon, Dr. Angela Clark, Ms.

Jenai Copeland, Dr. Idna Corbett, Dr. Jina Fast, Dr. Anita Foeman, Ms. Kathleen Groff, Ms. Alicia Hahn, Dr. Tammy James, Dr. Bessie Lawton, Ms. Lauren Lang, Ms. Erica Littles, Dr. Querida Lugo, Ms. Lillian Morrison, Dr. Katherine Norris, Dr. Cherise Pollard, Ms. Preeti Singh, Dr. Justin Sprague, Dr. Melissa Swauger, Dr. tonya thames-taylor, Ms. Chloe Webb-Barnes, Dr. Joan Woolfrey, and last but definitely not least, Dr. Hyoejin Yoon, who mentored countless women of color, me, this project, and whose powerful legacy will be felt for many generations to come.

Last and most, I thank my whole family, especially my son, Patrick, for just being himself: smart, thoughtful, kind, and for always, always making me laugh. He is the funnier one—100 percent.

Sam: I want to first thank all the women of color students I got a chance to meet and interview for their stories that informed this book. Y'all are so awesome!

I thank our stellar research team. Thanks to C. E. Brown and Christa Rivers, who taught me so much during my time working alongside them on the project. To Lisa, for her mentorship throughout my undergraduate career and beyond, and for the opportunity for me to be on her research team. To Odette, for her friendship and professional relationship that evolved from working on this project together as research assistants.

I want to thank my undergraduate university for providing the conditions for me to cross paths with Lisa and Odette. Our relationship has evolved over the years, and I'm so grateful that I got to work on this book with them both as co-authors. They have pushed me and made me a better writer as a result. I thank my professors who influenced me in so many ways for the better. I'm grateful to them for seeing my potential when I couldn't see it. I thank the scholars whom I've learned from and for the scholarship that informed our work.

I thank my friends for their support, interest in my writing career, and offers to take me out when I needed to get out of the house, and for hyping me up when I needed some encouragement. I'm truly lucky to have the most amazing tribe in my life.

I thank my family for their love and support. A special thanks to my mom and dad for the sacrifices they made for my sisters and me, and for instilling in us the value of education. I wouldn't be where I am today if it weren't for them. I'm grateful that even though they didn't always understand what I really did as a career, they were always proud to brag about it in typical Caribbean fashion.

I am grateful for my ancestors. I honor the legacy that I come from even if I do not know all of their names. I am their wildest dreams.

Lastly, I want to thank God, who continues to guide my path, provide me with opportunities to grow, and be there for me in ways I don't always realize.

Odette: I would like to start by thanking fellow members of our research team Lisa Huebner, Christa Rivers, Sam Jeune, and C. E. Brown for working so diligently on this project. I am forever grateful that I got to be a part of this journey with you all. To all our women of color students, this book would not have been possible without your insight and words of wisdom. You all are the true motivation for this book. Thank you so much for trusting us and allowing us to highlight your experiences.

I'm eternally grateful to my mom, who is one of my biggest inspirations. Mom, you came to this country from Liberia at the age of eighteen with a goal of creating a better life for yourself. Besides giving the best hugs, you have taught me love, kindness, discipline, respect, and so much more that has helped me to succeed in life. I truly have no idea where I'd be if it weren't for the sacrifices you've made for my sister and me throughout the years. You inspire me every day with your thoughtfulness, your care for others, and your unique sense of humor. I couldn't ask for a better mom. To Papa, Grandma, Auntie Mommy, Uncle Marc, Tony, Ashley, Alana, Zhi, Leion, Quincy, Morgan, and the rest of my extended family, I love you all.

To my twin sister, Ovette. My forever cheerleader, first best friend, and womb buddy, you are such a light in my life. From our long conversations, our love of K-pop/Asian dramas, to all of our inside jokes—you have been beside me through the good, the bad, the ugly, and everything in between. You are hands down one of the bravest people I know; seeing you navigate your autoimmune conditions (#lupuswarrior) with such strength and grace is beyond awe inspiring. From the womb to the tomb, I love you always.

BEST FRIEND!! Niccia, it still amazes me that we have known each other for over twenty years. I am forever grateful that you decided to be my friend the first day of fourth grade. With each passing year, you continue to teach me about the importance of friendship.

To my amazing boyfriend, Matt, thank you so much for your endless love, support, and patience. You bring such joy, laughter, and kindness to my life. Thank you for being a sounding board for all my ideas throughout writing this book. I am forever grateful to be on this journey called life with you.

To my amazing friends who have now become family: Jessica, Karl, Alpha, Ingrey, Laura, Abdul, Heba, and Donna, you all inspire me every day, and I am so grateful to have you in my life. Finally, I would like to thank God for his blessing and for bringing me though all my trials and tribulations.

Success at a Price

CHAPTER 1

Diversity Dilemmas

Whose Success and at What Cost?

Stephanie,[1] a Black woman college student, is worried, but she is not sure why. She's excelling in classes and life on campus seems to be okay, but a nagging feeling, a persistent tug, warns her that perhaps she made a bad decision to come to North Middleton University. Although close to several major cities, North Middleton is a predominantly white institution of higher education (PWI). She chose North Middleton because it seemed so diverse, but upon coming to campus, she regretted her decision. She keeps looking for other women of color, but she sees hardly any students who look like her, even fewer staff members, and still fewer professors. What Stephanie calls a "sea of whiteness" feels confusing, especially given how hard she works to belong. Even though she tries to cope by just staying quiet, listening, observing, and taking notes, she is exhausted to be one of only a couple of women of color in her classes, often the only Black woman, especially when conversations turn to race. But then sometimes she is compelled to speak because she isn't confident that her white professors will correct the white students.

Not sure where to turn, Stephanie decides to go talk to her professor. She's white, but she seems generally cool and supportive. Stephanie would rather go to a woman professor who is not white, but she doesn't have any, so she settles on this one. The professor's door is open. Stephanie peeks in and asks whether she has time to talk. The professor smiles at Stephanie, appearing happy to see her. She tells Stephanie to come in and gestures toward the seat in front of her desk.

Stephanie sits down, appearing a bit nervous and unsure, and she begins to explain her frustrations and concerns. Stephanie tells her professor that she knows she is doing well "on paper," but she still feels alone because she cannot relate to

---

1 Stephanie is one of the many research participants you will read about in this book. Unless otherwise noted, all names are changed.

most of her peers or professors. She says she often thinks to herself, "I can't be the only one," but she consistently feels isolated and like she doesn't belong, which doesn't seem right. Stephanie explains that even as she struggles, she is always trying to figure out how to make it better. But then she gets overwhelmed, stops thinking, and just tries to "push through." But then she feels guilty because when she pushes through, she is not standing up for herself or for her people. Stephanie talks with her professor for a long time. When she is finished, she smiles, thanks her, and says it was good to vent. She feels some relief, but she also knows it is momentary and not enough.

What invisible barriers do women of color students face while thriving on a campus that excludes them? Stephanie, like many of the college students you will read about in this book, was an outstanding student who was on track to apply to graduate school, professional school, and attain the job of her choice. She had a high GPA, consistently demonstrated significant campus involvement, and was well known for her achievements. Yet, despite her successes "on paper," Stephanie experienced persistent isolation and doubts. She internalized these feelings and sometimes blamed herself for having them. At the same time, however, she knew her emotions were bigger than herself and connected to her experiences of being at a (PWI). Although she had never talked with anyone else about these feelings, Stephanie suspected other students might also be thriving academically but hurting socially and psychologically.

A member of our research team, Christa Rivers (her real name), called this phenomenon "the daily normal." The daily normal, discussed in greater detail in chapter 4, explains how our participants experienced *and* mitigated constant, pervasive interactions that resulted from various intersections of racism, sexism, classism, homophobia, and xenophobia. These interactions were sometimes mundane, making participants feel dismissed and disrespected, and were sometimes extreme, causing them to experience discrimination and dehumanization. They occurred in the classroom, in student organizations, at university events, and in town. But a major part of the dilemmas outlined in this book is how the students felt deceived by North Middleton, which claimed to be a university that prohibited racism, sexism, and other identity-based oppression. Our participants knew they were attending a predominantly white university, but they also believed that they were promised a university that was much more diverse than it was, and one that would not tolerate clear systemic oppression. What's more, when they learned about this gap between the promises of diversity and the realities of oppression, many of these high-achieving students felt responsible for bridging this gap—for themselves, for other students of color, and ultimately for the university.

The Dilemma of Success

North Middleton University is a regional PWI that understood it needed to do some work to improve its diversity. At the time of this initial conversation with Stephanie, 81 percent of the university's undergraduate population was white. Like other institutions of higher education seeking to promote diversity, equity, and inclusion, North Middleton supported various programs to increase and support its underrepresented student population. One such initiative was formed to investigate the gaps in admissions, retention, and graduation among underrepresented students by studying their grade point averages, retention rates, and graduation rates over a period of three years. The study found gaps in enrollment, retention, and graduation for Black and Latino men, but no gaps for women of color, especially Black women. Instead, women of color were appearing to succeed on all fronts: high GPAs, graduation in four years, and significant campus involvement. Upon hearing this report, university administration responded swiftly by creating and funding programs to support Black and Latino men, but did nothing to learn more about the experiences of women of color.

These findings of success—based largely on quantitative measures like GPA and graduation rates—starkly contrasted with the stories told to us by Black, Latina, Asian, and multiracial students: that alongside their achievements, they were experiencing isolation and emotional and physical pain. Later, these initial anecdotes were confirmed by our research findings. Participants endured countless situations of simultaneous racism, sexism, classism, homophobia, and xenophobia as part of campus climate and navigated additional pressures imposed by the very projects designed to help them. Because success was measured by graduation rates and GPA scores alone, these struggles were invisible, which also made the strength and resilience of these women invisible. The problem was clear. On one hand, women of color undergraduates were being celebrated as institutional successes, which at first glance seemed positive. At the same time, however, they were being dismissed and underserved. As we discussed the report findings, we found ourselves asking, Who is succeeding here and at what cost?

To answer this question, we knew we also needed to critically examine how universities measure success and how they determine truth about it. Many of us in higher education are very interested in supporting students from a wide range of backgrounds, and are invested in ensuring that education is diverse, equitable, and inclusive. We rely on established academic measures and methods, many of which claim neutrality in assessing what we know to be true. However, social justice scholars and activists have long critiqued how the production of knowledge is not free from biases, and how truth—about a wide range of issues—is shaped heavily by dominant narratives that come from privileged groups and social and cultural norms. These privileged perspectives inform both the knowledge that comes from traditional measures and methods and the argument that they are bias-free. A critical view on traditional measures and methods makes clear that knowledge production—the production of truth—is an enterprise not unlike other social and economic enterprises. It, like others, is informed by social and economic power dynamics and sometimes reproduces them—even with the best of intentions.

Given this, we must understand social justice and equity issues from the perspectives of those who are closest to the phenomena we seek to address and remedy. In doing so, we help ensure that we consider the viewpoints in our explanations, our measures, and in our solutions that are not apparent in traditional knowledge making. If we only rely on established methods of knowledge making, we miss the most important pieces of logic—the pieces that do not come from books, but rather from life. In her renowned essay "The Master's Tools Will Never Dismantle the Master's House," Audre Lorde said it best: "Those of us who stand outside the circle of this society's definition of acceptable women; those of us who have forged in the crucibles of difference, those of us who are poor, who are lesbians, who are Black, who are older—know that survival is not an *academic skill*" (1984, 112).

Survival is not an academic skill, and it cannot be fully understood by means that are designed only by those in power. How women of color undergraduate students survive and thrive at predominantly white institutions of higher education and understand them must count as critical knowledge in any measure or method of diversity, equity, and inclusion. As we all develop our own measures and methods of diversity, equity, and inclusion, we should ask how women of color students both survive and thrive at predominantly white institutions of higher education, and how their knowledge about these experiences could help us.

The primary goal of this book is to improve the college experiences for women of color undergraduates by sharing what we have learned from them and their experiences in predominantly white universities. Their unique perspectives on diversity, equity, and inclusion complicate how PWIs tell stories about diversity and critique institutional efforts at spotlighting diversity success. Many PWIs might appear to be well intentioned in their efforts but remain ill prepared to understand the unique challenges faced by women of color undergraduate students. These misunderstandings result in part from narrow definitions of success that focus only on recruitment numbers, retention numbers, and GPA comparisons and fail to consider emotional and physical well-being. Misunderstandings also result from the ways that PWIs spotlight the successes of women of color students as measures for and messages of institutional diversity without consideration for what they've endured to thrive.

In this book, we refer to PWIs as institutions that are "well intentioned" to capture how even in the best case, diversity efforts can fail those whom they are trying to help. This is not to excuse PWIs for these failures, but to encourage all of us to dig deeper when creating diversity initiatives. We use the word "thrive" when referring to women of color undergraduates to emphasize their strength and resilience, but the term should not be read as dismissing the importance of our critique or erasing the difficulties they've experienced along the way. Thriving despite erasure and harassment and excelling with academic and cocurricular achievements should never be the sole measures of institutional success. Every university should celebrate its successful students, but when these same students feel ignored, alone, and deceived, they also feel exploited by the very university system that is dedicated to helping them.

Black Feminist Epistemology and Intersectionality Theory

To help explain the experiences of and insights from women of color undergraduate students, we draw on and contribute to the scholarship of Black feminist scholars, critical race feminist theorists, and those who use an intersectional approach. Renowned legal scholar Kimberlé Crenshaw initially coined the term "intersectionality" to explain how the experiences of women of color are erased within the workplace and the justice system, as they do not fit within existing lenses used to understand racism, sexism, discrimination, and justice (1989). For example, sexual harassment law considers sex discrimination and racial harassment law emphasizes race discrimination, but neither of these remedies harassments that combine multiple forms of discrimination (Crenshaw 1992). As an analytic lens, intersectionality improves former conceptions of inequities experienced by women of color that falsely add layers of oppression together—that is, "double burden," "triple burden," "multiple axes of oppression" (Jones 2015).

Crenshaw is credited for coining the term "intersectionality" to help women of color, specifically Black women. However, she has stated multiple times how the concept is part of a rich intellectual tradition that is rooted in the writings of women's and gender studies scholars from a wide variety of racial backgrounds, which have long demonstrated how identity is political and multiple identities interlock to form experiences of oppression and privilege (Anzaldúa 1987; Collins and Bilge 2019; Combahee River Collective 1983; A. Davis A. 1981; hooks 1984; Lorde 1984; Moraga and Anzaldúa 1983). The intersectional approach continues to be central in women's and gender studies in the United States and around the world (Berger and Guidroz 2010; Collins and Bilge 2016; John 2015; Mohanty 2003; Yuval-

Davis 2006). Intersectionality has also "traveled" in that it has also been theoretically developed and empirically tested by scholars and activists in a wide range of other disciplines, such as psychology (Cole 2009), political science (Hancock 2007), sociology (Collins 2000; McCall 2005), geography (Valentine 2007), and law (Williams 1992). In sum, intersectionality is a conceptual and methodological framework that explains how discrete social categories—race, gender, sexuality, class, and nationality—work together to create unique experiences of privilege and oppression.

It is important that we are clear that not only do we practice an intersectional approach in this research, but we also do so with a clear indication of its intellectual roots in women of color feminisms and Black feminist epistemology produced primarily by scholars and activists who are women of color. This makes no mistake about the theoretical undergirding from which we draw. We use intersectionality to help interpret the experiences of women of color, but Lisa, especially, could never speak for or on behalf of our participants. Intersectionality is a theoretical approach, one of the many developed by women of color feminists, but we do not use it for this reason (Nash 2013). Instead, we follow Black woman scholar Jennifer Nash and white woman scholar Kathy Davis, who have both expanded the potential of intersectionality and Black feminist thought while being accountable to their own standpoint perspectives. As such, they respect the raced-gendered bodies of the mostly women of color who produce Black feminist thought, but also call for the sharing of labor and travels of this theory (K. Davis 2020; Nash 2018, 2013, 2008). This frees Black women and other women of color scholars to produce a wide range of scholarship (Nash 2018) and allows for intersectionality to travel—that is, to be taken up and used, be critically considered, and be clarified across a wide range of projects (K. Davis 2020).

Not unlike other theoretical and empirical traditions with a long intellectual genealogy, intersectionality has seen its uses widely explored and its intellectual origins debated (K. Davis 2020, 2008; Nash 2018, 2008). This is in part why we—like Lisa had in her first book—see this work as a guide on how to use intersectionality as both a theoretical lens and a method (Ruchti 2012). This seems especially important for research in higher education, which has largely dismissed, misused, or altogether ignored the concept of intersectionality (Harris and Patton 2019). Additionally, it is important for professors and administrators in the humanities and social sciences who use intersectionality frequently to engage with its critiques and "alleged weaknesses" to be clear about how and when an intersectional lens best produces knowledge and informs policy and praxis. In this book, we demonstrate how an intersectional approach is essential to the conceptualization of the experiences, labor, and insights from women of color undergraduates. But we also show how to use intersectionality in research design that aims to promote social justice.

In the documentary *Cultural Criticism & Transformation* (Jhally, 1997), bell hooks describes how intersectionality is not just a lens to explain experience or to promote social justice. It also produces new knowledge: "An explicit goal of the intersectionality research paradigm is disruption. Intersectionality disrupts who is considered a reliable epistemic agent." We decided to use a theoretical frame that would honor these experiences and offer suggestions to the diversity dilemma in higher education. We use intersectionality to ensure the epistemic agency of self-identified women of color undergraduate students. We come from a Black feminist perspective to make clear the intellectual genealogy that frames this project, as well as to articulate our specific use of intersectionality.

Although we each continue to learn, study, and apply Black feminist epistemology, women of color feminism, and intersectionality, we do not claim expertise, nor do we adopt these theories lightly, or simply because they are foundational to women's and gender studies (Nash 2018, 2013). We do not have an allegiance to intersectionality per se. Rather, we follow Black feminist sociologist Dr. Patricia Hill Collins, who teaches us how intersectionality frameworks yield knowledge claims that are critical to social and political praxis broadly (1999). In other words, neither singular nor additive frameworks work to fully explain the experiences of women of color, but more than this, we assert that singular and additive experiences do not fully explain any phenomena. Therefore, we have used intersectionality throughout this project to frame questions, to collect data, and to inform analysis by seeing which categories emerge as thematically salient in varied and in particular contexts.

The Study: Feminist, Ethnographic, and Intersectional

We combined an intersectional lens with institutional ethnography to develop the ideas in this book with and on behalf of self-identified women of color undergraduate students as they understood their experiences in a predominantly white, public, regional university. Institutional ethnography is "research for the people" because it emphasizes the perspectives of the people who are most affected by the phenomena studied, but it also considers the roles and relations of power that are organized by the institutional setting in which the experiences occur (D. Smith 2005). It is empirically rigorous because it triangulates several forms of data collection and analysis to test the salience of thematic findings (D. Smith 2005).

Our study included three years of observation at campus events (2014–17), in-depth interviews with forty-five self-identified women of color undergraduate students, and content analysis of university print and digital promotion and recruitment materials. It was also informed by a university-wide mentorship program several university staff and faculty had designed to support women of color college students and to learn more about their experiences with education. Fourteen college students were assigned a faculty/staff mentor and matched with high school mentees. The program lasted one year and included many formal community-building activities such as bimonthly meetings and topical workshops, service projects in the community, and kickoffs and send-offs. We also facilitated and encouraged informal connections through regular check ins, a digital presence, and suggestions for activities and events. Faculty and staff mentors conducted unstructured recorded interviews with the college students, and then the students did the same with their high school mentees. As a team we continuously assessed the results of these activities and considered next steps. One of these was to conduct additional research to further explore and explain the experiences of women of color undergraduate students in a predominantly white, public, regional university. This program was highly successful, and all participants wanted it to continue.

Our findings from the three-year study illuminate how well-meaning institutions of higher education do not support high-achieving women of color students and inadvertently exploit their successes in the name of diversity and inclusion. They also make clear the daily struggles and obstacles that women of color students must overcome and how they do so. Last, the findings show how women of color experienced these struggles differently in ways that emerged as thematic patterns, with some identity-based categories being more salient than others in particular contexts. For example, most participants experienced gendered-raced harassment from their peers—white people of all gender identities and men of color—but how these harassments occurred varied. Biracial women reported how their peers consistently asked "what are you?" and how these interrogations felt both mundane and invasive at the same time. Black women did not hear these objectifying questions, but their identities were also scrutinized, which made them feel "boxed in" in ways that corresponded with controlling images of Black women (Collins 2000).

The Dilemma of Diversity Work

To explain how even well-intentioned institutions of higher education inadvertently harm the very students they are trying to help, we combine theories that critique the use of diversity and other identity-based initiatives to further the corporatization of universities with theories of emotional labor that help explain how institutions profit off workers' management of emotions. In *On Being Included:*

Racism and Diversity in Institutional Life, Sara Ahmed asks, "How does the will become a wall[?]" when exploring dilemmas faced by diversity workers in institutions of higher education (2012). We use this question to frame the experience of women of color undergraduates in relation to this dilemma, asking how the will of even well-intentioned PWIs becomes a wall of barriers and obstacles faced by women of color students. Many institutions of higher education communicate diversity as a goal, but this is not enough to ensure that diversity is integrated as a practice, especially when the labor of communication involves—and potentially exploits—women of color students.

To help reveal and explain this exploitation of women of color students—even that which is described as unintended—we return to sociological theories of emotional labor first coined and explained by sociologist Arlie Russell Hochschild. As Hochschild explains in her landmark study *The Managed Heart*, exploitation occurs when employers require care and service workers to manipulate their emotions in ways that increase customer satisfaction but are unpaid labor that then increases profit. This work contributes to corporate profit at the expense of the employee because it is invisible, unrecognized, and unpaid (1983). The concept of emotional labor has been tested in a wide variety of research studies about various types of work that regularly employ care and service to ensure customer satisfaction (Hochschild 2003; Ruchti 2012). There is also a growing body of literature that uses emotional labor to explain inequalities in higher education by focusing on how the bodies of faculty of color become objectified as "diversity currency" to further profit the institution (Musser 2015). Until now, however, no book has used emotional labor to explain the experiences of women of color undergraduates and simultaneously critique neoliberal approaches to diversity, equity, and inclusion.

The Authors: Standpoint Epistemology

A central tenet and practice in women's and gender studies, sociology of gender, and related disciplines that commit to the pursuit of social justice is for researchers/writers to consistently interrogate the relationship between our identity-based experiences and the research process, and that relationship's effects on participants. One way to do this is to claim our own subjectivities, our own standpoint perspectives, and consider how these perspectives inform the research we design and the knowledge we produce (Blee 2000; Collins 2000; Harding 2004; Nash 2018; D. Smith 1990). Each team member was involved in every stage of the research from design through analysis, and we each considered how our identities shaped our research design, data collection, and analysis throughout (Collins 1986; Twine and

Warren 2000). None of us took our identities for granted, and we were mindful about the identities of the team we developed. What follows is a brief statement from each of us that explains our standpoints and how they relate to this project and to this book. The next section details how we negotiated these different standpoints as researchers and writers in ways that also prioritized the perspectives of our participants.

Sam: I identify as a Black Haitian American woman. As in many Caribbean families, education was the most important thing in our household. It was to be achieved by any means necessary. I was to take advantage of the opportunities afforded me here as a natural-born citizen and go further than the generation before me. Like several of our participants, I, too, attended a predominantly white institution because I knew I could not attend my HBCUs of choice, as they were too far from my parents and too expensive. Knowing my options were PWIs close to home, I made sure to find a school that had some level of diversity because I didn't want to feel like the only Black person in the room. Coming from a diverse high school where most of my friends and classmates were people of color, I hoped to have some aspect of that environment in college.

During my undergraduate career at a predominantly white institution, I navigated three worlds: Haitian culture, Black American culture, and white dominant culture. I had to negotiate the traditional cultural values that I grew up with and the more progressive and "American" values that I was exposed to and adopted (to a certain extent). Additionally, I sometimes felt disconnected from Black American culture because of my upbringing. While pursuing my education, I experienced guilt (Covarrubias and Fryberg 2015) because I had an opportunity that many in my family did not have. I felt the pressure to be the best and prove that my parents had not made all these sacrifices for nothing. However, I also wrestled with the belief that I was betraying my culture and family to advance myself in society.

That's how I found my way to women's and gender studies. Although I was on the path to becoming a pediatrician (a culturally appropriate career), classes in women's and gender studies showed me that becoming a doctor wasn't the only way to positively impact the lives of others. I wanted to understand and address the social, political, and economic injustices that create barriers in marginalized populations' lives. My coursework in women's and gender studies showed me that my lived experience is one of knowledge production. However, the courses I took gave me language for the things I've experienced in my life—like intersectionality, systemic oppression, and institutional bias. These concepts I already understood these concepts based on my personal experiences but didn't have the vocabulary to describe them before. I also took feminist research methods classes that then provided me the tools to apply in this research, such as intersectionality and standpoint theory. These provided a framework for the research project that complemented the knowledge from my lived experience.

I recognize that my identities shape how I view the world, and I cannot be fully removed from the work. To some extent, I was aware that I was positioned as an insider based on identities that participants also claimed. As a participant-researcher, I identified with several of the experiences that participants described, creating moments of camaraderie between us during interviews. However, I knew that my experience wasn't everyone's, and I had to be mindful of my bias when an experience did not match mine. Although I do come from marginalized identities, I tried my best to not assume that I would know or understand everything our participants shared.

During the research, themes arose that I didn't expect. Even though I am from a marginalized group, I also have privilege. Interrogating one's privilege is important to see how it can affect one's approach to the work. I might have been positioned as an outsider by participants because I was working as a research assistant for a white woman professor employed at a PWI. As we stated earlier, our participants had every reason to distrust the primary investigator and the research project itself (Zinn et al. 1990; Zinn 1979). So my insider status as a woman of color college student might have only gotten me so far due to my proximity to whiteness.

Odette: As a first-generation American born to two African parents, I have had to navigate various intersecting establishments that include gender, African / Black American culture, and white society and ideology. In my academic career, I have often struggled with principles instilled in me at an early age. Like many African families, my family stressed the importance of education and always working hard. It was not enough to "do well." I needed to excel, as I was representing not only myself, but my family as well. Throughout my undergraduate career, I felt the pressure of this duty. This responsibility became burdensome; I even crafted my entire career by the standards I knew would make my family proud. For me, this meant majoring in biology to fulfill a prestigious medical career. Throughout my first two semesters as an undergraduate, I recall feeling massive anxiety because I believed that I wasn't being true to myself in favor of pleasing my family. In contrast, I also thought that by becoming a doctor I was honoring the sacrifices of my extended family and mother, who primarily raised my sister and me alone.

The importance of proximity to American culture (whiteness) was another foundation stressed by my family. As a result, I often struggled to connect with Black culture. My relatives frequently discussed the differences between African/ Black communities and white society. Common themes that came up in these conversations included praising the white community for its ability to succeed and prosper while Black individuals were often called lazy for not obtaining the same levels of success as their white counterparts. At an early age, I began to understand the properties of racism, xenophobia, classism, and so forth, and how they shaped the ways in which people of color are viewed. I thank my mom for educating my sister and me about these concepts, but also for introducing us to different cultures and communities. Her doing this helped pique my interest in social justice, equity, and inclusion. It wasn't until I took my first women's and gender studies class that I began to believe that I had the language and tools to articulate my feelings, systemic systems, racial bias, and white supremacy.

My degree in women's and gender studies has been invaluable to me in both my professional and personal life. I have been interested in having a career in health care, and throughout my undergraduate years, I gained the knowledge to discuss the various ways in which gender and other inequities affect an individual's treatment and participation in the medical care systems and other institutions. Through courses like Gender, Race, and Science, I was able to expand on my knowledge of concepts surrounding institutional bias and build a framework to navigate health research and program design.

My identities and background have had a vast influence on how I see the world and the ways in which I continue to show up to do this work. As a participant-researcher, I gained much insight about women in my community. Regardless of our backgrounds, we all shared an array of commonalities that showed up in our research. During the analysis phase of the study, many participants discussed feelings of isolation and erasure. Listening to their interviews, I felt a connection with these women, as I often dealt with similar emotions throughout my academic and professional career. At times, it was heartbreaking to hear these women speak about their experiences attending a PWI. I also felt privileged that I was able to witness their growth, strength, and success even as they navigated these institutions. In addition, while working on this research study, I was challenged by having to address many of my beliefs and biases that I had formed throughout my life.

Lisa: I am a white American woman from a small midwestern town. I was raised by a family that believes in equality, hard work, and the power of education. It was expected that I would go to an affordable in-state college, be able to take care of myself, and, ultimately, make a positive difference in the world. All my communities have been primarily white, and all of my schools have been predominantly white institutions. As a white person in predominantly white institutions and communities, I felt an ease that I did not recognize until I considered the perspectives of people of color and learned about theories of privilege and power (McIntosh 1988).

I attended a state university approximately twenty minutes from my hometown. Although this was a PWI, it was here that I found a home in two interdisciplinary programs: women's studies and ethnic studies. In these classes, in large part because these programs were merged as a cost-saving measure, I benefited from learning about women's studies from varied racial, ethnic, and transnational perspectives. I became acutely aware of my whiteness as an area of privilege and "blissful ignorance." Women's and gender studies gave me language to understand my own experience as a white woman and the experiences of women of color. Women's and gender studies continue to help me articulate the relationship between identity, personal experiences, and social, political, and economic life. I will never forget the day I realized that my whiteness had detrimental effects despite my good intentions as an individual. It also dawned on me that it was a function of white supremacy that I did not have to consider whiteness until I was nineteen years old.

Fast-forward thirty years, and, as I tell my students, I still work to mitigate my identities in the pursuit of social justice. Sometimes I succeed, but often I fail. I don't say this to garner sympathy or to accompany any white tears. I say this as an empirical fact. Consistently failing is a condition of social privilege, and the only solution is to see it, own it, and try to remedy it. A lot has stayed the same in thirty years about the basic dynamics of oppression, privilege, and power. However, a lot has also changed. As a lifelong student of identity politics, I find it amazing to observe how people claim identities to name themselves in authentic, honorable ways that also contribute to knowledge. For my students of color, I strive to be more than an ally and instead work toward being an accomplice feminist who rejects saviorism, embraces anger, and strives to be accountable (Kendall 2020).

As I continue to consider the relationship between my standpoint positionality and the work I produce, I am grateful for the epistemic contributions of my students, our research participants for certain, and the student researchers on this project especially. To begin, I appreciate C. E. Brown, the first student on the team, the only other white person who helped me to consistently interrogate my own whiteness, for their analytic insight and steadfast attention to detail, especially in the beginning stages of the project. Next, thanks to Christa Rivers, the first participant-researcher on the team as both a woman of color student and research assistant, for her acute observations, connections, and insights that pushed all our thinking further. Last, this project—and the richness of this book—would not have been possible without the intellectual labor of Sam and Odette, first as my students, then as student participant-researchers, and now as my colleagues and cowriters.

All of this said, the irony is not lost on me that this project would not have happened without the emotional labor of women of color, and that although they were paid, their labor was far from fully compensated. I would be remiss if I did not acknowledge this inherent tension in the work: how any of my own intellectual contributions have depended in large part on the emotional labor of these women of color.[2] Although this is a tension perhaps without resolution, it is one that can only be visible through the acknowledgment of one's standpoint, especially in relation to the scholarship we produce.

We/They: Insider/Outsider Knowledge and the Question of Shared Authorship

While each of us is equally committed to social justice and to this project, we also come from different standpoint perspectives. As part of our commitment to consider how identity-based power dynamics informed our research and the knowledge it produced, we join several traditions in sociology, women's and gender studies, and other related disciplines, which have considered the influence of researcher race and other identity-based experiences on research methodologies and participants.

On one hand, given the profound and persistent production and effects of social inequalities, social justice scholars have argued that "racial matching" between researchers and participants fosters the safest space for understanding the experiences of marginalized subjects (Zinn et al. 1990; Zinn 1979). At the same time, sociologist ethnographers have made clear that insider status is not always enough, especially when seeking to explain the experiences of those closest to oppression (Twine 2000). For example, "race-matched" interviews and observations sometimes yield partial data in part because participants assume mutual knowledge with researchers of shared identities. As a result, participants do not always articulate what they assume is "common knowledge" related to shared identity and instead say something like "well you know what I mean" (Twine 2000). Gaps in knowledge can also occur because shared cultural norms prevent disclosures, especially disclosures about sensitive topics (Twine 2000). In addition, there is wide variation of standpoint perspectives within racial groups, which means that shared race does not mean shared class, gender, nationality, or sexuality experiences. These differences require an intersectional lens to ensure that analysis is specific and not reductive (Berger and Guidroz 2010).

Given the different but complementary benefit of both insider and outsider perspectives in the pursuit of social justice knowledge, we believe that a careful consideration of the relationship between standpoint perspectives and the production of knowledge yields the idea that perhaps both insider and outsider perspectives help facilitate the broadest and most comprehensive understanding

---

2   I sincerely thank my colleague Dr. Justin Sprague for making this last point and helping me see it and articulate it here.

of power dynamics related to oppression, privilege, diversity, inclusion, and equity. Thus, we integrated our consideration of shifting insider, outsider, and insider-outsider perspectives as part of the research and writing process, not because one standpoint at any given time was particularly better than another, but because they each offered different views that helped to inform what we understood to be true (Twine 2000).

Throughout the study, we each paid close attention to the kinds of data that we culled from interviews and participant observations, especially noting whether, how, and when race matching and other identity-based matching between researcher and participants affected the process (Twine 2000). We wrote qualitative memos to document these identity-based influences and analyses individually and discussed them as a team. We included these insights in our coding tree, memos, and other analytic tools. Some themes were deductive, informed by previous scholarship. For example, Lisa did not take her identity, especially as a white woman professor, for granted in this intellectual pursuit, as her whiteness likely afforded her privilege through what Jonathan Warren calls an "imagined superiority of whiteness" (2000, 161). At the same time, and although race matching does not guarantee trust (Blee 2000), our participants had every reason to not trust her or the research enterprise (Zinn et al. 1990; Zinn 1979). As women of color undergraduate researchers, however, our participants might have been more likely to trust Sam and Odette as insiders (Collins 2000). Some of this analysis was inductive—for example, how both Sam and Odette noted that they were often positioned as outsiders to participants due to multiple intersecting identities, and because they were assisting a white woman professor.

In our dissemination of all our findings, but especially in this book, our goal has been to consider the influence of our varied standpoint perspectives, but in ways that also emphasize and center the perspectives of our participants. We follow the traditions found in decolonial feminist theory, specifically those of renowned philosopher Maria Lugones, that have created critical space for empathetic understanding found in what she calls "world traveling," "shared consciousness" and "complex communication" (which we extend to analysis and activism) that do not dilute or erase identity-based relations of power, oppression, and privilege (Lugones 2006, 1987; Lugones and Spelman 1983).

Following decolonial feminist philosophers Maria Lugones and Elizabeth Spelman, we also "write together, but not as one voice" (Lugones and Spelman 1983). In their renowned essay "Have We Got a Theory for You! Feminist Theory, Cultural Imperialism, and the Demand for the 'Woman's Voice,'" Lugones, a Hispana, and Spelman, a white/Anglo woman, explain how and why they wrote one article together, with shared knowledge of truth, but without assuming one unified voice in relation to the experience of that truth:

> In the process of our talking and writing together, we saw that the differences between us did not permit our speaking in one voice. For example, when we agreed we expressed the thought differently; there were some things that both of us thought were true but could not express as true of each of us; sometimes we could not say 'we'; and sometimes one of us could not express the thought in the first person singular, and to express it in the third person would be to present an outsider's and not an insider's perspective. Thus, the use of two voices is central both to the process of constructing this paper and to the substance of it. *We are both the authors of this paper and not just sections of it, but we write together without presupposing unity of expression or of experience (italics ours).* So, when we speak in unison it means just that there are two voices and not just one. (Lugones and Spelman 1983, 573)

Just like our research, our writing is coalitional, and it reflects our combined analytic voice in pursuit of social justice. Like Lugones and Spelman, we are also shared authors of this book, "and not just sections of it." Moreover, we "write together without presupposing unity of expression or experience." Through writing together but not as one voice, we seek to preserve individual standpoint perspectives, center the experiences and knowledge of our participants, and preserve the potential for shared transformative practice.

Throughout the writing of this book, we have each hoped to create a story that centers the standpoints of our participants, all self-identified women of color undergraduate students. While writing together, we also hoped to preserve and honor our specific positionalities (Lugones and Spelman 1983). As a result, the reader will notice that some language will sometimes shift accordingly. For example, the reader will sometimes read "we" in reference to other women of color, and at other times the reader will read "they." This is not meant to be confusing, but rather to preserve the authenticity of each of our different intersecting identities, which inform each of our writing voices. We are telling this story together, but at the same time, we hope to safeguard our different perspectives and lived experiences throughout.

Goals for the Book and Remaining Chapters

Our goal for *Success at a Price* is that it will improve the lives of women of color undergraduate students at PWIs, assist professionals who aim to do the same, and contribute to scholarly, policy, and practical discourse. The rest of this book will tell a new story of successful women of color undergraduate students, revealing invisible barriers, demonstrating how they overcome them, and providing their recommendations to higher education administrators and policymakers. A combination of theories that are typically discussed separately—intersectionality, emotional labor, and critiques of neoliberal conceptions of diversity—will help contextualize and explain these stories, which we hope will advance practice and policy on the ground. Each chapter will include specific discussion of how to apply and model intersectionality in a higher education setting.

In Chapter 2, "'You Are Welcome Here': Failed Promises," we analyze the disparities between what North Middleton—as an example of a PWI in the United States—offers and what high-achieving women of color undergraduate students experience. To begin, we learn how PWIs strategically and purposefully recruit students of color. We explain these recruitment patterns as interpreted by women of color undergraduates and analyzed by us to show that they are both well meaning *and* misleading. These experiences of deception and disappointment are exacerbated when the institution highlights the successes of a few students of color, but neither addresses clear systemic inequities in academic and student affairs, nor offers substantive help in response to the students' needs, as defined by them. We draw on and synthesize theories that critique neoliberal universalizing diversity initiatives, intersectional theories of space and place, and theories of emotional labor to situate the perspectives and experiences of women of color undergraduates in broader systems of inequality.

Chapter 3, "'I Want to Say Something': The Price of Bridging Labor," explains and contextualizes the specific burdens experienced by women of color undergraduates when they are positioned to be a "bridge" of communication and education to further institutional diversity initiatives and goals. This bridge manifests itself in several ways and in various contexts: in the classroom, in student organizations, in university promotion efforts, with white peers, with and on behalf of men of color peers, and for faculty, staff, and administrators. We explain the historical legacy of this burden by drawing on the renowned collection *This Bridge Called My Back: Radical Writings by Women of Color* and other Black and women of color feminist scholarship. We use the intersectional approach to show how and when specific identities merge that contribute to this burden to make clear that these burdens are socially experienced and systemically caused. We use emotional labor theory to explain how "being a bridge" is work that is uncompensated, unrecognized, but also promotes the university. We synthesize Black feminist theories, intersectionality, and emotional labor theory to frame and contextualize this invisible labor and the effects on women of color undergraduates.

In Chapter 4, "'What Are You?':The Daily Normal," we explain how women of color undergraduates experience racism, sexism, homophobia, and xenophobia, as explained and interpreted by them. While these may be analyzed as microaggressions, we use the term coined by Christa Rivers, "the daily normal," to capture how women of color undergraduates consistently mitigate offenses that are simultaneously mundane, extreme, and normalized. Women of color also mitigated experiences of disrespect from peers, faculty, and staff who asked invasive, inappropriate questions and violated their personal and bodily space. Women of color experienced dehumanizing incidents of harassment and other forms of violence in social media, on campus, and in town. We analyze all of these through an intersectional lens to help explain and contextualize specific harmful acts so that they can be more visible in diversity discourse and remedies.

Chapter 5, "'Assume Whatever You Want about Me, but Let Me Blow Your Mind': Successes and Strategies," gives voice to the power, agency, and resistance of women of color undergraduates to demonstrate *how* they successfully navigated college, not just that they did. It details specific strategies that emerged as themes from the data, advice these students would offer to younger women of color, and suggestions for institutional and policy change. We analyze all of these within the rich tradition of Black feminist scholarship that aims to highlight the struggles, the survivals, and the knowledge gleaned from identity-based experience.

The last chapter, Chapter 6, "Diversity Solutions: Redefining Student Success," turns our attention to the theoretical and practical uses of this book developed from the knowledge we have gained from women of color undergraduates. Theoretically, we hope this unique synthesis of intersectionality, critiques of neoliberal diversity initiatives, and emotional labor will be applied in other studies of inequality in higher education and elsewhere. We also hope this book will model how the intersectional approach can be used to study higher education to best explain the experiences, labor, and insight gained from the perspectives of women of color undergraduate students. Practically, we hope this book will serve as a guide for higher education professionals and anyone else interested in complicating diversity narratives and strengthening diversity initiatives. We should all consider these perspectives, take up these recommendations, and honor the experience and knowledge offered by these amazing students.

CHAPTER 2

"You Are Welcome Here"

Failed Promises

A three-minute video begins with a university president holding a sign with the handwritten message "#YouAreWelcomeHere." He introduces himself and says that the university welcomes "students from nations all over the world," telling them, "Your presence enriches our campus." All following scenes show faculty, staff, and students, speaking various languages, some for themselves, some on behalf of their departments, each holding the same sign, each repeating the same words: "You are welcome here." The emphasis is on the people, who appear diverse in race, gender, and age. Some identify as students, some as faculty, and some as staff. Some scenes have one person, and some have many. The instrumental music in the background is light and upbeat, which evokes a positive and hopeful feeling for the viewer. The video ends with one last frame of the university name and logo.

A video very similar to this one was produced at North Middleton during our study. Our participants reported that many students were frustrated at the university's claims, mostly because they were unaccompanied by real action. Research assistant Christa analyzed the film as follows:

> This video tokenizes staff and students of color. The video attempts to demonstrate diversity, pushing the "you are welcome here" message over and over again while not offering evidence of concrete ways students of "diverse" backgrounds will be supported. Sure, students are welcome here . . . but how will we support students when they face racism on campus, when they are ostracized or otherwise excluded from groups of white students in their dorms, treated as invisible/made hypervisible in their predominantly white classes, stopped by white police for driving while Black, followed around a store in town, questioned by Immi-

gration and Customs Enforcement on campus. To my last point, in an age where immigrant students are especially vulnerable, we must do more than make students feel welcome. Students need material, emotional, and social support, none of which this video mentions. This message is a sham.

Like Christa, many of our research participants felt deceived, primarily because they were promised a welcoming, diverse campus but had to endure being unwelcomed at North Middleton. How predominantly white institutions aspire to attain diversity but simultaneously deceive students of color is one of the diversity dilemmas outlined in this book. Under the worst conditions, this deception is purposeful and part of a neoliberal marketing strategy to gain capital. Under the best conditions, this blind spot is unintentional and invisible via assumed whiteness, masculinity, and other identities of privilege. The intentions do not matter, however, because in both cases the outcome for women of color undergraduates is the same.

That women of color undergraduates felt alone, deceived, and exploited is not what North Middleton administration wanted. They wanted all their students to feel safe, welcome, and at "at home," but the promotion of diversity intentions combined with the absence of process made women of color undergraduates feel worse. A major part of North Middleton's equity activities was to ensure that international students felt safe and included on its campus. This video was designed to convey this message, but its primary purpose was recruitment, with a focus on presenting an array of diverse bodies, not on the provision of structural supports.

How is it that North Middleton promised diversity, but our participants felt deceived? In this chapter, we explain how the institution's white, masculine, elite, and middle-class spaces provided a foundation for North Middleton's diversity, equity, and inclusion efforts, which ultimately failed women of color undergraduates. The university did not acknowledge these failures publicly. Instead, the administration consistently marketed diversity as success measures, which were defined primarily through individual outcomes. This neoliberal approach to diversity helped to increase capital gain for the university.

Neoliberal approaches to diversity, equity, and inclusion focus on individual difference without attention to structural power. This is in direct conflict with equity because an "all difference matters, in all contexts, inclusion for all" application of diversity, equity, and inclusion privileges those already in power at the expense of those who are not. Our participants discovered this conflict when they looked for the diversity they were promised at North Middleton but did not see themselves. They not only felt disappointment in this lack, but they also felt deceived. When they looked closer, they saw how so much of campus life was segregated

by race and other identity-based experiences that contradicted the university's assertions. In other words, participants' seeking of the diversity they were promised
yielded observations and experiences of white, masculine, elite spaces that were
contrary to the claims made by North Middleton.

Norming White, Masculine, and Elite Spaces

In her book *Space Invaders: Race, Gender, and Bodies out of Place* (2004), Nirmal
Puwar explains the problems that occur when institutions "prove" diversity solely
through an increase of different bodies: "It is assumed that, once we have more
women and racialized minorities, or other groups, represented in the hierarchies
of organizations (government, civil service, judiciary, police, universities, and the
arts sector), especially in elite positions of those hierarchies, then we shall have diversity" (1). That there needs to be an invitation to belong is not just an effort to
increase diversity; it is also evidence of a silent but pervasive norm. Claims of wel-
comeness also demonstrate what is assumed but not seen: that the universal body
of leadership and belonging is the body that is white, masculine, and elite. Puwar
terms *this* body and the implication of belonging the "somatic norm."

The somatic norm is constructed in part by hegemonic ideologies that situate dominant white masculinity as a logical, civilized, unemotional "non-body"
against a foil of illogical, savage, and overemotional bodies of women and people
of color. These are further supported by other intersectional ideologies and practices that ultimately support patriarchy, white supremacy, colonialism, and capitalism. Thus, the logical, unemotional non-body of elite white men are justified
in their dominance to "protect" white elite women in the name of nation, civility,
and advancement. To support this, white elite femininities are only valuable inas-
much as they are fragile, submissive, and in need of protection. This same norm
justifies white supremacy and colonialism by simultaneously exoticizing and dehumanizing women of color, and by "protecting" all women from men of color
in ways that serve white supremacist imperialism. The somatic norm is both un-
marked and everywhere, which universalizes a logical, unfeeling non-body. This
assumption is possible because the normed body is invisible, an assumption that is
present but fades in the background. In contrast, women and people of color are
created as deviations of this norm, as othered, which helps to preserve the norm,
the assumed but invisible background (Collins 2000).

We first recognized how our participants experienced what was promised to be
a diverse campus through their observations of the high numbers of white people
everywhere they looked. For example, Mary, a biracial (Black and white) woman,
said, "I know it's a diverse campus, but I do see a lot of white students here." Ari, a

Black woman, agreed: "There were significantly more actual white people on campus than what was presented in campus promotional materials. The website lied because it is totally different from what I saw. I don't feel comfortable enough to call North Middleton home." Many of our participants expressed this same sentiment early in the interviews—how the large quantity of white people countered their expectations for a diverse campus and made them feel like they did not belong.

Some participants specifically chose a predominantly white institution (rather than an HBCU) because they were looking for diversity. For example, Carol, a Black woman, explained, "My aunt said I should have gone to an HBCU but I didn't want to go to one, why should I have to? I didn't want to because one, they are really expensive, and two, why must I go to an HBCU because I am not comfortable? I shouldn't have to be around people who are my own skin color to be comfortable. I should be comfortable wherever I go. It shouldn't matter."

Whether or not they specifically sought a PWI, all our research participants expressed the same sentiments as Carol. Each wanted to be part of the environment she saw online and in print images—one that explicitly had equal numbers of people from a wide variety of racial, ethnic, and gender backgrounds. They wanted to see themselves, but not just themselves. They wanted what they considered to be true diversity—a place that had equal representation and opportunity—but as they began to assimilate to campus life, their expectations of inclusion shattered. Rather than a campus that was populated by relatively equal numbers of people from a wide array of racial backgrounds, these undergraduates experienced a campus that was dominated by white people. People of color were situated in isolation or in small numbers. When there were large numbers of people of color present, they were concentrated outside major events and apart from the wider campus community.

Instead of feeling safe and "at home," our participants encountered a campus that felt uncomfortable to them. As Tina, an African American woman, explained, "North Middleton is for the white people. We're kind of like the lost Cocoa Puffs in the Cheerios because there's no one in here of color." It wasn't just that participants felt unwelcome, but also that they knew white people were welcome. As bodies outside of the somatic norm, our participants knew they did not belong, but they also knew the people who did. As women of color students, they identified who was centered on campus, and it was clear they were not.

People of color confirm diversity through seeing similarity—other bodies of color—not by seeing difference from others (Ahmed 2012; Anderson 2022). Our participants discovered the somatic norm at North Middleton in part by looking for other people that looked like them. When diverse populations mix in an already white space, white people see difference and change, but Black people and people of color see sameness and familiarity. As Anderson explains, although white people do not have to look for themselves in white spaces, Black people and other people of color consistently look for themselves as part of entering and settling into a white space (2022).

When asked what she might advise a new woman of color college student, Jackie, a Black woman, replied, "I would tell them, know that what you see is not at all what happens, but they're good at it. They had it on the front page. 'We are building up equity, academics, and diversity.' I laughed so hard. Where? There are white girls here and a sprinkle of Black people in this picture. Like what are you doing?" As part of survival, existing, and thriving, women of color undergraduates had to continuously assess the level of whiteness in the same spaces that white people simultaneously saw as normal, expected, and mundane. As a result of seeking sameness, they also began to see how North Middleton excluded them and normed whiteness.

"The Look"

In seeing so many white people on campus, our participants identified the somatic norm. All other bodies in the space are assessed against the somatic norm. They are in the space but not quite of it, not quite integrated as within. Instead, women, nonbinary people, and non-whites are simultaneously hypervisible and invisible when the assumed, and therefore visible, body is white, masculine, elite, or middle-class. Puwar explains this simultaneous invisibility and hypervisibility by describing "the look" that women and people of color experience as they dare to move through spaces not normed for them. Nonverbal and usually communicated through facial expressions, but also through other body gestures, "the look" conveys varying sentiments of surprise, shock, and contempt to women and people of color who enter spaces that counter the somatic norm. "The look" that occurs in everyday interactions on the ground contradicts the welcome message that comes from the highest echelons of the institution. "The look" ranges from disrespecting and dehumanizing to dismissing and doubting. Whether seen or not seen, women of color undergraduates are "looked" at differently from their white and men of color peers.

Our participants' feelings of unwelcomeness and unbelonging at North Middleton occurred in part because they also felt "the look" when they encountered white peers on campus. Consider this conversation between research assistant Christa and Kaliyah, a Haitian woman participant, about walking through and sitting in the student union:

KALIYAH: There were no Black people there. I was reminded that I was a Black person. And it's uncomfortable and you feel like attention [is on you] because even though they're not seeing it, you can, you can sense who is thinking something about you because you're Black.

CHRISTA: I totally understand. I felt that sitting upstairs waiting for you to come meet me. I was sitting there. And there's like a table full of white men. I saw their letters. So I don't like those. I don't take white fraternities and sororities seriously. Because they are a joke but just sitting there. I could feel some of them staring at me. And I didn't make any type of eye contact with them. Because they're not worth my time.

KALIYAH: Exactly. Exactly.

CHRISTA: Anyway, so you felt reminded of your Blackness.

Christa and Kaliyah's conversation demonstrates the pattern of feeling consistently seen and not seen that was reported by many of our research participants. Exchanges like these are exemplary of how women of color experience the coupling of being hypervisible and invisible that results from being in a white, masculine, elite space (Ahmed 2012; Anderson 2022; Evan-Winters and Love 2015; Evans, Domingue, and Mitchell 2019; Puwar 2004). The experiences of "the look" were not isolated moments. They were ongoing, occurring in a wide variety of spaces and persisting over time. As a result of looking for themselves, women of color undergraduates quickly and consistently noticed the somatic norm. As a result, they also noticed how hypervisible they became to white people who were noticing them. This is a tension that people of color feel in a white space—being both invisible and hypervisible at the same time.

"Have I Had a Black Teacher Yet?"
White Classes and White Teachers

One of the most salient white spaces at North Middleton was the classroom. As Kaliyah explained, "There are not that many African Americans in the class, for the most part they are white women and for the most part they are my age, 20, 21, 22, they are no older than 23 years. In Physics, it is pretty well balanced as far as male and female, but it's not diverse there, it's mostly white people. [How does that make you feel?] For the most part I am accustomed to it at this point." Many participants discussed how they knew that North Middleton had more white people than people of color in general, and how they expected to see more white students in class. Still, participants also reported that they felt uncomfortable about these conditions.

How our participants understood the somatic norm at North Middleton did not make it easier for them. For example, Dawn, a Black woman, explained that she still felt discomfort each and every time she entered a classroom, despite being a senior at North Middleton: "Yeah. It can, it can still feel really awkward just walking into a classroom and being the only Black person there, it can still feel really isolating being the only person of color in the room. I think in most of my classes, I was probably the only Black person in the room and then going to junior year, I was probably like the only Black person or Black woman in the room and fast forwarding to this past year." Dawn expected to see white people but still felt that uncomfortable jolt of recognition each time she was the sole Black person in the space. Sociologist Elijah Anderson explains this realization as knowing you are looking at a "white space" when you consider predominantly white institutions of higher education (2022). As he instructs, one of the most persistent indicators of racism and white supremacy is how white people consistently avoid spaces considered Black at the same time that Black people cannot avoid white space (Anderson 2022).

For white people, white spaces are just spaces. Even with the best of intentions, whiteness is normed as the default, as a space without race. When white people enter predominantly white institutions of higher education, they notice nothing different. When Black people and other people of color enter these same spaces, they immediately feel difference and know they've entered a space "they are required to navigate as a condition of their existence" (Anderson 2022, 13).

Participants had to consistently navigate their classrooms as white spaces for several reasons, but one overwhelmingly salient theme was how low numbers of faculty and staff of color made it more difficult for them. They knew that there could have been more such faculty and staff, but that North Middleton did not make hiring and retaining such employees a priority. As Dana, an African American woman, explained:

> I feel like faculty needs to be distributed a little more evenly when it comes to race. I'm trying to think—have I had a Black teacher yet? No, I haven't had a Black professor yet. That's sad. That's not ok. I really don't see diversity among the faculty at all. Unless you get diverse faculty in here, students won't be as comfortable and outgoing, and vocal, about their needs, wants and opinions. I think that is something that needs to be improved. Because I have my advisor now who is a white woman and I think she's really helpful but if I had a Black woman in that space, I would feel more comfortable and just to help with my path and if I see her do it then I think I can do it. If we don't have role models, like they say, if you don't see it, how do you think you're going to be it? I really feel like that's true. I

know for me, I really want to teach on the college level but if I don't see professors that are Black and female, how the hell do I think I'm going to do it? And I do feel doubt and discouragement when I think about my path because I don't see it, like don't Black people teach college? It's a shame.

Despite their long-standing intellectual, programmatic, and administrative contributions to the academy, women of color faculty and staff continue to receive little to no institutional support when compared with their white counterparts (Evans-Winters and Love 2015; Evans, Domingue, and Mitchell 2019; Gaëtane and Lloyd-Jones 2011; Gutiérrez y Muhs et al. 2012; Yenika-Agbaw and Hidalgo de Jesus 2011). Thus there remains an unfair distribution of faculty of color, as Dana rightly notes above. This is generally unjust, but the lack of Black women faculty specifically worsened the college experience for our participants.

The lack of Black women faculty was disappointing to our participants, but they described how the dominance of white faculty, even well-meaning ones, had detrimental effects as well. Tina explains how she knew her white professor only "saw" her because she happened to be wearing a suit in class one day. She attributed this recognition to how this clothing seemed apart from stereotypes of urban Black women:

> It's like, a lot of times, I feel, especially when I don't try to have a relationship with my professors. Like, talk to them. Really. I feel like that stereotype is automatically, just there until I see otherwise. Like, especially if I don't participate in class, I don't speak too often. I remember one professor I had. And one class I had come back from a job interview. So I was in class, dressed up, I was in a suit. And that's the first time she ever acknowledged me in class. And she was, she's like, 'You know what? I've seen you in class.' And I'm thinking, 'No, you haven't.' And she said, 'You've been doing such a good job. And you seem so interesting. I want you to be on my research team this summer.' And I just looked at her and I'm like, no, it's just because I came in and I looked not like the typical, Black girl in the classroom. And I speak properly all the time. Like, that's the only reason why you acknowledged me. And I'm just another face in the crowd. So like, there's very few, there's a handful of teachers that like, I feel see me for me, like I'm not like just some Black girl in the class that speaks well and that's presentable all the time. And, like super professional, they actually have a name instead of just characteristics.

Like many of our participants, Tina felt invisible to her professors because she thought she didn't fit the image of the stereotypical urban Black girl they expected. Yet if her demeanor had happened to match stereotypes or false controlling images—as you will read about in chapter 4—she would have been hypervisible and dismissed, disrespected, or dehumanized. Our participants consistently reported how they believed their professors—most, if not all, of whom were white—were influenced by negative stereotypes and therefore biased. This experience is part of what makes a space white, masculine, and middle-class, and, as Tina said, is "automatically there until I see otherwise." Although promised otherwise, our participants immediately noticed the somatic norm at North Middleton. They also knew that navigating these spaces was necessary for them to graduate, but that they were harder for them to experience than for white students.

Feminist scholar Sara Ahmed explains how predominantly white institutions don't see the negative outcomes of diversity initiatives because of "permanence of whiteness" (2012). The permanence of whiteness is a social condition that is rooted in white supremacy and manifested in everyday circumstances, even those that aim for inclusion. These circumstances are usually assumed for and administered by white elite men and then solidified as a universally applied institutional practice. People of color notice these practices as exclusionary to them, but as is the case with all social privilege, this exclusion is invisible to white people, especially those who are in power.

Ahmed's explanation of the assumptions for whiteness, the norming of whiteness, or what she calls the "permanence of whiteness" can help explain the gap between our participants' experiences and North Middleton's intentions. As Ahmed instructs, it is important to examine diversity communications and content to increase our understanding of what is not said as much as what is said. To communicate about difference means we must first notice what is different, but as Ahmed reminds us, noticing difference tells us "more about what is already in place than about what is new" (2012, 35). For example, "if diversity is something that becomes added to organizations, like color, then it confirms the whiteness of something already in place" (Ahmed 2012, 3). This alone is not a bad thing, but coupled with the question of purpose, it becomes clear that diversity communications also demonstrate that people of color are not the norm. Through this lens, the very presence of diversity content makes clear the implicit and assumed foreground of whiteness.

Universalizing White Women to All Women

Puwar and Ahmed further explain the impact of white, masculine, elite spaces when white people enter and then remain in areas that are clearly meant for people of color (Ahmed 2012; Puwar 2004). The fact that white people persist in staying—or, as Ahmed describes it, "sink in" to a space—despite several verbal and visual reminders that a place is for people of color demonstrates how white people (even if they are the only ones) feel comfortable and welcome where they are not even meant to be.

For example, when a group of North Middleton women of color students created programming specifically for themselves, and when a white woman student complained about not being allowed to access that group, administrators fought the initiative by stating that any student programming for women should include all women, regardless of race. Faculty, students, and staff challenged this decision, which resulted in its reversal and support for the programming just for women of color. At the same time, how this turn of events required extra effort on behalf of women of color students is evidence for how PWIs norm inclusion as inclusion for all, which ultimately privileges the already privileged. It also makes clear the extra and invisible labor required from women of color undergraduates, labor that ultimately supported the university's DEI efforts.

That North Middleton administrators supported a white woman student who had complained because she could not participate in a group specifically designed for women of color is evidence of the university's white, masculine, elite permanence that universalizes the dominant group to all groups. Administrators had insisted that any student programming for women should include all women. Both the student's and North Middleton's *grip* to the space, even space that was clearly marked as non-white, is evidence for how whiteness was made central and normed as an assumed expectation. It also provides evidence of the constant labor that people of color must do to create a separate space for themselves in the first place.

Even the most well-intentioned PWIs fall short when they fail to consider the normed assumptions that are informed by the universality of whiteness and other identity-based privilege. This is especially notable when we consider what is not being said when diversity is announced or encouraged. We are told equity and inclusion are the outcomes when a PWI asserts diversity, but what assumptions foreground these assertions? Under what conditions is inclusion being asserted? Under what conditions is it not? Who has access to equitable conditions and who does not? North Middleton supported the white woman complainant in the name of inclusion; however, the administration clearly missed the mark because doing so failed to support women of color students. Diversity and inclusion efforts do not promote equity when the outcome is to support students who already have access over students who have less. North Middleton changing its mind is a good sign that demonstrates how its intentions were perhaps good. At the same time, however, this reversal is evidence for the permanence of white, masculine, and elite spaces, and for this permanence's invisibility to administrators unless explicitly addressed by faculty, staff, and students.

White, Masculine, Elite Spaces: A Neoliberal Strategy

The permanence of white, masculine, elite spaces is also revealed when analyzing how the language of diversity is used as a descriptor to brand and market the institution. Marking institutions as neoliberal makes clear the structural benefit that universities gain from diversity and inclusion efforts. Henry Giroux argues that in systems of global capitalism, no social institution is immune to the dominance of market forces, including the university. He and other scholars define neoliberalism as an ideology that guarantees freedom, but only through successful participation in the market. Success within a neoliberal framework is defined, then, not by contributions to the social good but rather by increases in economic profit.

As part of neoliberalism, universities focus on individual aspirations and successes, not collective solidarity and community gains. Through neoliberalism, there is less emphasis on the political and more emphasis on the private and the personal. Because common patterns across and among groups are minimized at the expense of individualism, definitions of success are taken from the experiences of the dominant group (because part of having power is the ability to be heard) and then universally applied, regardless of structural difference. For example, the dominant group in society might have the perspective that people can succeed if they just work hard enough, but this is problematic when this perspective is uncritically applied to all people. Further, neoliberal ideas sound promising and attractive to people who have less control over their social and economic circumstances. Wouldn't it be great if all it took to succeed was hard work? As a result, hegemonic practices and policies are designed and implemented with the accompanying discourse that promises inclusion for all, but only benefits the elite.

How does neoliberalism affect diversity initiatives at a university? The neoliberal university redefines diversity by changing it to difference, which includes discussion of human variance that is disconnected from discussions of power (J. Alexander 2005; Mohanty 2003). In this context, then, all differences matter, all perspectives matter, in all contexts. Postcolonial transnational feminist scholar Chandra Talpade Mohanty calls this a "flattening of difference" to argue that when all differences matter equally in all contexts without an analysis of power, no differences matter at all. This erasure occurs, according to Mohanty, because neoliberal universities dilute the potential of transformative change, which leads to social justice, by erasing the specific and precise perspectives of disenfranchised groups. Since its primary purpose is capital, the neoliberal university promotes scholarship and programs that emphasize individualism, which ultimately makes radical knowledge—and its potentially transformative power—disappear.

Critiques of neoliberal universities make space for radical knowledge that emphasizes the processes, practices, and effects of systemic power relations. The focus on diversity as strategies shows how predominantly white institutions reproduce the very thing they want to change when they aim to increase admission and graduation of underrepresented minority students via a variety of earnest recruitment and retention efforts (Ahmed 2012). These are institutions that have a clear record of goals *and* outcomes, such as emphasizing diversity in strategic goals and visions, branding themselves as diverse institutions through marketing and admissions materials, participating in equity assessments, and allocating funding for diversity research, programs, and staffing. Although many of these institutions appear to have good intentions, they are still part of the neoliberal regime in higher education. The trend of neoliberalism in universities makes clear that the means—a postsecondary education—yield a very specific end: contributions to the market. This is not necessarily the same as the end desired by those of us invested in social justice, where the means—a postsecondary education—would yield contributions to the common good.

There is a significant history in how diversity, inclusion, and equity programs have been developed to support neoliberal aims. Indeed, as critical race and queer studies scholar Amber Jamilla Musser (2015) notes, women's studies and ethnic studies emerged while universities were recognizing and investing in diversity. These events occurred during and because of the civil rights movements in the 1960s, which were influenced by students on college campuses seeking to make change in the world by starting at the university level. However, rather than integrating these lessons in revolutionary ways that would disrupt structural and epistemological functions, the university took advantage of this rhetoric to use "difference" to increase profit. This profit is masked by neoliberal rhetoric (i.e., multiculturalism) that celebrates diversity and inclusion, but neither addresses the specific needs of people of color nor acknowledges the harm endured by their bodies.

Over time, this early focus on difference evolved to language concerning diversity, equity, and inclusion. This shift broadened the emphasis of diversity of race and ethnicity to include other identity-based experiences of gender, sexuality, and nation, but still drew on ideologies of individualism and color blindness associated with neoliberalist access to power. Today, many universities conflate structural inequalities with diverse perspectives so that all diversity is equal diversity.

This was certainly the case at North Middleton during our research study. On one hand, North Middleton demonstrated its diversity through marketing and branding content, especially images and language designed to recruit students. At the same time, however, we found a consistent pattern in interviews and in observations that showed how North Middleton adopted neoliberal language in its DEI efforts and other university-sponsored initiatives. Over time and in a range of programs, discussion facilitators consistently exclaimed that "we are all diverse." They cited students' political party, geographic location (i.e., coming to North Middleton from out of state or in state), and other identity factors not linked to access to power. What were mere cultural exchanges were marked as initiatives that increased recruitment and retention but did not result in improvements. This was exacerbated by well-meaning departments that sought to hire people of color because they valued equity and inclusion but then did not consider what it meant to retain them.

After North Middleton conducted a series of equity studies, the university instituted programs to help men of color undergraduates, but the specific needs of women of color unfortunately remained invisible. While the North Middleton study helped to celebrate the successes of women of color, the administration did not capture the *process* of this success—for example, how women of color are succeeding and at what cost to them (or to others). In addition, relying only on these quantitative measures resulted in institutional strategies that ignored the needs of women of color.

Diversity Speech Acts

One way to dismantle white, masculine, and elite spaces is to consider how diversity, equity, and inclusion strategies are deployed as tools to maintain the neoliberal university. Let's begin by interrogating North Middleton's claims of diversity, equity, and inclusion as accomplishments. Institutions that promise that diversity has been attained must also prove it. Predominantly white institutions of higher education show that they are diverse by counting people of color: establishing the number of recruits, graduates, successful alumni, and events. They demonstrate these diversity accomplishments through public declarations, communication, and content, what Ahmed refers to as "official institutional speech acts." She explains, "Diversity utterances would thus be verifiable statements; they could be measured in terms of their truth value. The utility of equal opportunity data can be understood at least partly in terms of how data can be used to test the validity of diversity as a constative utterance" (2012, 55).

Like many predominantly white institutions of higher education, North Middleton prided itself on being diverse, and it would consistently communicate this diversity everywhere: through images on the website, in the media, in admission materials, and in publications. These images provided proof that the claims of diversity in the university mission and strategic plans had been accomplished. Countless committees, initiatives, programs, and curricula promised and promoted diversity in ways that would then promise the result of inclusion and equity.

Institutional leaders make claims about diversity in relation to other university goals to demonstrate excellence (Ahmed 2012). These claims exaggerate fairness and cohesion because they are designed to support the accomplishment of other objectives (J. Alexander 2005; Mohanty 2013, 2003). Highlighting diversity in relation to how it assists institutional goals fails to consider the value of diversity on its own, only measuring its value against objectives implicitly considered foundational to the success of the institution. Although diversity derives its value primarily from its use for other goals, it does provide a path for communication. This path is limited, however, if the scope of communication is only celebratory or for recognition. This aim—of recognition—does not provide a reference point from which to respond and intervene when trouble arises. This avenue of communication also becomes stagnant if the word "diversity" is overused as a buzzword because it fails to make meaningful structural change. As Ahmed warns, if "diversity" is only used to describe an institution, it is more likely to sustain the structures of the institution than to challenge and change them.

North Middleton conveyed its diversity to the broader community through its web pages, pictures, and videos, but the fact that this content existed as highlights made clear the university's overall foregrounding of elite white masculinity (Ahmed 2012; Puwar 2004). Predominantly white institutions of higher education that claim to serve people from a wide variety of backgrounds must work to diversify their student bodies for both ideological and economic reasons. Our participants noticed and were attracted to how official speech acts of diversity appeared everywhere in North Middleton's content: in its commitments to missions, goal statements, accomplishments, and strategically placed images of diverse bodies. Jane, a Black woman, explained the specific diversity speech acts that drew her to North Middleton: "They have multicultural organizations, but all those organizations don't really get funding at all so to keep it going, it's kind of like their own passion. Then coming here and doing tours and stuff, statues in the middle of campus and it's like wow this school is actually big on diversity and making people feel included but it's kind of like a token more than anything."

Like many of our participants, Jane noted how North Middleton demonstrated its symbolic commitment to diversity through language, images, and statues. But once arriving on campus, she quickly saw how these were relatively empty promises due to lack of funding and other types of structural support. Many women of color undergraduates who confirmed Jane's experience shared the specific visuals that drew them to North Middleton, but simultaneously made clear how these masked what was a permanent white, masculine, elite space (Ahmed 2012; Puwar 2004).

Participants knew the diversity claims were false in part because they did not see themselves on campus. A closer and retrospective look at the website also revealed that they did not see many people of color. When they did, they saw people of color presented in specific marginalized ways that still centered the campus as a white masculine space. Consider the analysis of Jillian, a Black woman who was initially drawn to the university:

> Now that I'm thinking about the website you never see pictures of events when the crowd is predominantly people of color. Like the rally at homecoming, we had a whole bunch of people at the rally getting excited for homecoming, encouraging people to come and vote, you didn't see any pictures of that on the page. You never see pictures of the large number of students that are studying in the multicultural lounge or students who are working in the multicultural lounge or projects by the multicultural lounge—you never see that on the home page.

Veronica, a Black woman, agreed that the day-to-day operations of the multicultural center were left out of university promotions: "You never see pictures of the large number of students studying in the office of multicultural affairs or students that are working in it or the seminars that it has, you never see that on the home page." Several other participants noted the same pattern—that the website and other university materials highlighted people of color in a series of images, but did so in ways that centered white activities as mainstream university activities. There were few to no images of programs or events that were created by people of color.

As participants began to describe the gap between the promise from North Middleton and their own observations on campus, they also explained how they felt betrayed. Many explicitly chose North Middleton because they saw so many images of people of color on the website. At first they felt secure, but over time this security changed to anger and feeling tricked. Dana explained this shift:

> I feel like it's not diverse at all. I feel like you guys have a little bit of diversity, but you are not diverse enough to be claiming you are a diverse campus. It's not true at all. If it was diverse, I feel like I would see people mingling but it's not that way at all. You see big groups of white and the little group of Black or the Latino whatever. You're not seeing the mixture or the intertwine. And if your faculty doesn't look like that, how can your students look like that? I feel like that's false advertisement because when I came to North Middleton, I was expecting to see just different faces and I was shocked to see so many white people. I feel like it's for white people, everything they stand for, everything that is good, is for white people.

North Middleton promised "a home away from home" to its students, but our participants did not feel like they belonged once they arrived. Part of what the somatic norm, white permanence, and other analyses of white masculine spaces reveal is how white people don't notice how their whiteness distorts meanings of diversity, equity, and inclusion. "A home away from home" on a white foundation is only experienced by those students who are white. In contrast, our participants did not feel safe or secure, and these feelings were exacerbated when they realized the institution had deceived them. Jillian sums it up well:

> It is so interesting. I feel like that all the time though. Anytime you see a commercial or anything, it's always like one individual that's not white. [That] North Middleton claims to be diverse is frustrating because it is not diverse and that is something you don't understand until you get here, which is unfortunate. I think the university likes to say oh yeah, we're diverse to get students here but we don't really act on that diversity. It's one of those empty claims. I think that we have a lot of ways to go in terms of diversity. And I think the websites really make an effort to be like yeah, we need to really have those slideshows of people of color to make sure they know that we are not an all-white university when in fact it seems like that when you are here. The websites make an effort to highlight people of color but when you get here there is not a lot of faculty of color here but they could do a lot more to reach out to get faculty of color here but even like the staff, a lot of the staff you see of color, they work in the food area. You know when there is a lot of other jobs on campus that isn't just designated to food services. You never really see that many individuals of color outside of those roles. So, we are not as diverse as they make it seem.

As Jillian notes, diversity is demonstrated by the presence of people of color, but only in university marketing content. It is not demonstrated by the presence of people on North Middleton's campus, like faculty. White, masculine, elite permanence is further evidenced by Jane's and other participants' observations of how the institution failed to support efforts created by people of color as central to its operations. This has two effects: (1) programs that were produced by people of color, especially students, are marginalized, and (2) people of color, especially students, experience disproportionate pressure and responsibility for diversity, equity, and inclusion goals. White, masculine, elite permanence as a concept helps us make visible the other side of this power dynamic: the university programs that are funded as an ongoing part of operations and are centrally integrated throughout an institution.

A Segregated Campus

While we were analyzing university websites and other content, we were also analyzing our participants' experiences with this content. It was clear that there was a gap between what our participants hoped for before coming to campus and their experiences upon arrival. Close analysis of interview transcripts and meeting notes revealed patterns of segregation in residence halls, student activities, classrooms, and other university spaces. If asked, administrators at North Middleton would say that there was no evidence of segregation, and that segregation would be a direct violation of the university mission and goals. Initially, we didn't expect to see patterns of segregation. We found them because they were observed by our research participants, who then reported them to us. It was the looking for and the not finding of diversity that yielded these observations. In other words, these findings emerged only because the promise of diversity had failed women of color undergraduates so much that they looked around them and saw not only a white, masculine, elite space, but also one that they experienced and generally named as segregated.

Like many of our participants, Carolyn, a multiracial (Black and Latina) woman, explained how her discovery of a segregated university felt like normal campus life: "Eventually what happens is that a lot of times students segregate, like the white people with the white people and the rest of minorities with minorities, like at parties, it's just the way the cookie crumbles." Dana agreed:

> It was different. I mean the white people, they don't really want to get to know you, I mean they have their own functions. It's different. I feel like North Middleton is for the white people to be very honest, I think, I mean that was how it was in the beginning because I was a freshman then and I don't know everything going on, on campus. From the looks of everything, it looked like everything was for the white people and I was like ok, what do the Black people do? And that's when I got involved in multicultural orgs and it was kind of like ok, we have our own thing. I mean it's sad to say, I don't want to say that North Middleton is segregated, but you do see white people have their functions and then when it's the Black people functions, that's where you go. I definitely think in the first year it was hard to see that—it was all these white people, and you don't know where to fit in and I never dealt with white people. They were not being rude, but they were not being welcoming.

It was true. North Middleton prided itself on being welcome to all and offered many multicultural programs to accomplish this. What administrators failed to consider was that because these were offered to the entire university community, our participants believed that these programs were still primarily for "all the white people." Campus materials confirmed our participants' interpretations. For example, while the multicultural center stated that the main purpose of its programs was to "promote the success of students of color," its mission at large was to provide an "inclusive campus experience for all students." The intention of inclusivity for students is positive, but in a society that stratifies itself by race and other identity-based experiences, dominant groups would be privileged by default. In these cases, even the few spaces that are meant to be safe for students of color became white, masculine, elite spaces.

Segregated Housing

Our research team's in-depth interviews yielded observations and insights from participants that pointed toward systematic segregation in several university units, but especially in residence life and student affairs. Our participants considered some of these instances of segregation symbolic, but some could also be attributed to decisions made by the university that had structural effects. Many segregated activities were exacerbated by North Middleton's neoliberal approach to diversity: an overemphasis of difference that was unaccompanied by an analysis of power (J. Alexander 2005; Mohanty 2003). We initially learned about the pattern of invisible segregation from one of our first research participants, a Black woman named Veronica. She said,

> So, when I first got to North Middleton I saw the divide immediately. . . . Finley Hall was the Black dorm and I lived right next door, in Darrow. And I came in and everyone was like "oh, my friend lives in Finley, Finley, Finley, everyone lives in Finley and so I was like, "why does everyone live in Finley?" and they were like, "Oh, when you go through the academic development program over the summer, they put you in Finley so when you come back you just go to Finley. So, I say okay, so I go to Finley and Finley, they call Finley, the projects of North Middleton. All students call it that, students of color, not of color, it was just the thing.

As Veronica explained, all students labeled Finley "the projects" due to its concentration of students of color, especially students who did not meet the admissions criteria but had participated in programming designed to help them succeed at North Middleton. Calling Finley "the projects" is a clear nod to historical stratification that still occurs in the U.S. housing market, which separates Black spaces from white spaces (Anderson 2022). That this was not university-sponsored segregation mattered little. Finley's nickname and reputation as a "Black dorm" appeared as segregation to our participants. The dormitory served as a visible space that helped to solidify the invisible somatic norm of North Middleton as white, masculine, and elite (Puwar 2004).

Our participants' perception that housing was racially segregated was exacerbated by ideologies related to class, and the ways in which class intersects with race in U.S. society. Allie, a biracial woman, offered, "One thing I would say with traditional [dormitories], which is crazy because I guess it comes with people that have money and people that don't have money and you get the vibe with traditional that it is a lot more chill, and you see a lot more people of color. It's sad in a way, you know something that costs less has more people of color and something that costs more has more white people." Allie's analysis speaks to the broader theme in our research that identifies a clear racialized and classed divide between "traditional" housing and "new" housing at North Middleton. Many participants talked about how there seemed to be more people of color in the less expensive dorms. They understood this phenomenon not as a random act, but as an illustration of how housing was unfairly and disproportionately divided at North Middleton, which furthered their feelings of not belonging and being unwelcome on campus.

Segregated Greek Life

Segregation in housing was unpleasant, but our research participants described this circumstance as largely symbolic. It did not have major structural effects. This was not the case for how segregation occurred in fraternity and sorority programs, especially those that involved recruitment and retention. Veronica explained,

> And, um, so my freshman year, I had gotten involved with my sorority, I met them and I was like, oh, that's cool, Greek life is cool, but even, at the involvement fair; no, before the involvement fair, I was looking into Greek life, and I thought why not and like there's an ice cream social, where it's marketed to you like "sorority ice cream social" like so you think the sorority you want is going to be at the ice cream social and you pay ten dollars and you do your little bio and you go. So, we go to this ice cream social, and I'm looking, and I'm looking for the historically Black sororities, just to see if they're here. And there's like, um, Phi Mu, and there's Alpha Sigma Tau, and there's this group and that group and I'm like, okay, where are the Black girls? And, um, they were not included. The historically Black sororities were not in this round of recruitment. They weren't in this; they weren't in this type of recruitment at all.

Upon arrival in North Middleton, Veronica knew she wanted to join a historically Black sorority, and because the university had promised diversity, she assumed that all sororities would be present at all functions. The ice cream social was advertised as one for sororities, so she expected all of them would be there. That the ice cream social excluded Black and Latina sororities cannot be attributed to the existence of Black and Latina sororities to begin with. Such an analysis would be reductive and white supremacist, because it would blame communities of color for a structural decision made by a predominantly white institution. To be clear, the segregation resulted from the university-sponsored office, not from the fact that there are fraternities and sororities specifically devoted to communities of color. These organizations are part of a long legacy of solidarity, support, and uplift in a society that has and remains white supremacist.

Upon realizing that the ice cream social consisted of only white sororities, Veronica began to look for Black sororities. In doing so, she began to look for herself:

> And so, I was wondering, like, well, where do we find them and they were like, "Oh, at the involvement fair, you could find them." So, I go to the involvement fair, and there was literally, no lie, a row of Black and Latino Greek organizations and you had to go down this specific road to find them. The other sororities were kind of like surrounding the space, and they were kind of like in the intermingling space. And I was like, that's weird! [laughter] So then, um, from there, the divide came up again, like, okay, even Greek life they're separated. So, I was like okay, I don't want to be on one side of the fence or the other, I want to be able to sit in the middle and go where I want to go, so I went home and that was cool.

The involvement fair happened at the beginning of every semester at North Middleton to help students promote their activities and recruit members to organizations. Hundreds of groups and clubs decorated and staffed tables all day with the hope of attracting the thousands of students who might stop by between classes. How Veronica noted that the Black and Latino Greek organizations were "down a specific road" and away from the main activities "surrounding the space" is a clear description of "knowing when you are looking at a white space" (Anderson 2022).

Rather than include all sororities in recruitment activities that were designed specifically by fraternity and sorority affairs, North Middleton relegated Black and Latina sororities to a substantially larger event. This made it more likely that they were simultaneously lost in a "sea of whiteness" and hypervisible in stark contrast to the norm. For women of color undergraduates, the involvement fair was not "just a space." It was a space where they immediately felt different and then had to "navigate [this difference] as a condition of their existence" (Anderson 2022, 13).

Segregation in fraternity and sorority activities did not stop at recruitment. Veronica discussed her ongoing observations:

And then, um, in my dorm, um, I had lived with another woman of color and a white woman, they were my roommates. And we would notice how like, at first I was in a group of mixed people, it was Whites, Blacks, we were all together, and then as the school year kind of progressed, we kind of started to separate because it was kind of just like they were going to the White fraternity parties and we were going to the Black fraternity parties, and it was just really weird, how like, um, going to that house and going to this house. It was just very strange.

Here Veronica describes how her initial experience of segregation in Greek life helped her to explain other types of segregation between students at North Middleton. As a research team, we began to analyze the relationship between how the university falsely claimed its spaces as diverse and how students then separated themselves in other spaces. Did the university excluding Black and Latina sororities from initial sorority recruitment activities have other lasting effects? Were there other ways that North Middleton promised that fraternity and sorority life was equitable when it was not?

Our participants who were involved in Black and Latina sororities explained the importance of numbers in membership recruitment. It was university policy for organizations to maintain a certain number of members and recruits to be considered active. This blanket rule applied to all fraternity and sorority organizations, whether they were affiliated with Panhellenic and interfraternity groups, or with Black or Latino Greek life. It was well known at North Middleton that Panhellenic and interfraternity organizations were much larger than Black and Latino ones, but the university did not take this gap into consideration. The same number of new members was required regardless of current numbers of membership. For example, if a Panhellenic sorority with seventy members had to recruit twenty members to stay active, a Latina organization with fifteen current members had to do the same.

Carolyn explained how many students in Black and Latino organizations worked to fight this unfair system:

We talked to everybody. Waste of time. We talked to above her. Waste of time. You're complaining but nobody's listening. He listened, but nothing happened. Go to student government, make a major presentation, and said your requirement to have five people is racist. It is a racist policy. I broke it down, gave them the percentages of how many people in general are multicultural, have a 2.5 GPA, are interested, and this cuts it down a little bit more. When I broke it down, we have the sororities literally fighting for 50 potential girls. I expressed to your concerns, you agree that it is valid, but you do nothing about it.

Carolyn's frustration with and disappointment in student government leadership was echoed by other research participants, especially those who had decided to join student government to help make change.

Segregated Student Involvement

As one of only three senators at the time that were people of color, Ari, a Black woman, explained that many students of color did not want to get involved in student government because they did not feel welcome or that it was for them. This was understandable in a predominantly white institution, but it was also the reason Ari decided to run and get elected. As she said,

> So, there was always like, in the Black community, a lot of people didn't want to get involved in SGA. Because they feel like they're not welcomed. I don't know. Well, that's why we should be in it. So, it was just myself and my friend, but they gave us assigned seats because they didn't want us sitting next to each other or that type of thing. They personally gave everyone assigned seats, so it was obvious, but we were like, we're going to play it off. So, of course, we see it, but we just started texting each other each Tuesday night if we were not sitting with each other and kind of planned what we said in the meeting because they wouldn't let you speak more than twice on the topic.

How Ari and her friend strategized behind the scenes helped them "change a lot of things" because we were "on senate at the same time." These changes included making sure that the white senators understood why students of color from various ethnic backgrounds needed organizations just for them.

When Afro-Caribbean students wanted to form their own group, white senators suggested they join the Black Student Union. It was Ari and her friend who explained that this approach would be insufficient and inequitable, that the nuances of ethnicity and nationality more than justified a separate group. In addition, Ari and her friend explained why general rules would not work for organizations that were designed by and for students of color. Ari explained,

> What struck my last nerve was when the student government set a quota for how many people you need to have before you get removed. So, the historically black fraternities and sororities are dear to me, because I have family who were brought up in that environment. So basically, the student government was trying to set a quota for how many people you had to have in your organization before you got removed from campus and Greek life. But the student government doesn't allocate funds to any Greek life, right? So, it was like, you're not really doing anything. So how can you pull the plug on a group that you're not supporting? So, this was

crazy. And, like I said, there's only three people of color on this Senate, and our voice wasn't being heard.

So, we were trying to say, you know, to be a part of a Greek organization, you have to not only go through your campus, you have to go through nationals. And it's a process, it is a long and drawn-out process, and not everyone makes it. They don't rush, like, IFC. It is by invitation only, but it's through the relationships that you build. It's whoever's interested, we take you. That's how it goes. So, we had to explain that to them. But even after the explanation they didn't want to hear it.

It was not just that student government leaders "did not want to hear it"; it was also that they were able to enforce this silence by limiting the number of times each senator spoke. As Ari said earlier, "They wouldn't let you speak more than twice on the topic." Only the two senators of color had articulated concerns about this rule.

This did not stop Ari and her friend. They decided to partner with organizations outside of student government to ensure that their concerns were heard. Together with several multicultural student groups, they planned a "minority day of silence" that recruited students of color across campus. They created and distributed T-shirts that students wore, cards they could present to their professors in class, and materials that directed them to "meet at 3:15." At 3:15, all those who had promised silence convened in one of the most visible public outdoor spaces on campus before heading over to the student government meeting. Ari recalled,

So, we got t-shirts and that whole day, minorities pledged to be silent. And you know, get a little card if your professor is calling on you and all that good stuff. But you also wear your shirt and the shirt said at 3:15. You know it goes down. So, at 3:15 we were going to meet in the student union, and we were going to talk about everything. It was more so like a big rally like this is what we're doing. And we were going to walk together to the [student government meeting]. The meeting. Wow. Right. So, we did. And there was a whole bunch of us, we couldn't even fit inside. So, we went outside. And the look on everyone's faces. And like that's all we said, we didn't tell anybody anything unless you were already a part of, you know, unless you already had the inside scoop you didn't know. All you knew is 3:15. And then when you were there, we're like this is what's going on, on our campus. This is how we feel about it. This is what's happening. And, ultimately, when we got there, because remember, they put a ration on another student of color senator and I, we could not talk more than three times. But then with everyone there because it's open to the public. Everyone was talking. This is why you can't do it. This is why you can't do it. So, you couldn't ration a whole group of people speaking. And we got them to change. You know, the bylaws. So that the minimum number doesn't apply to the Black and Latino Greeks on campus.

The problem of segregation is not that people separate themselves, especially because people of color often must create non-white-only keep people of color spaces to equalize a white space. Segregation results in inequity when identity-based separation supports systems of oppression, or when rules that govern the group with the most power are uncritically and disproportionately applied to everyone, which then oppresses groups with less power. The minority day of silence was not protesting the existence of different groups. It ensured that minority voices were heard in a space that was otherwise characterized by a white, masculine, elite permanence. As a result, it—this collective of students of color—made structural change that helped Black and Latino fraternity and sorority organizations, but also furthered the university's diversity, equity, and inclusion goals.

The Success Story

Although a success and legendary tale talked about for years following, the minority day of silence was not reported by North Middleton, nor was it celebrated as part of the university's diversity, equity, and inclusion accomplishments. This lack was noted by our participants and by us. We analyzed such invisibility against our observations of how North Middleton promoted diversity, equity, and inclusion. In some of these celebrations, our participants felt like they and their friends had become success stories and poster children for the university.

These students appreciated the opportunities and recognition they received in publications and through social media, but they also felt conflicted. They worried that their own personal stories might contribute to false promises of diversity. They didn't, in the words of one, "want to mislead others like how I was misled about diversity on this campus." Many feared they were promoting "a lie." Jillian, a Black woman, explained, "I feel like it's a lie. I don't know, I kind of feel like a token Black child, like when something is wrong or something is going on like BLM [Black Lives Matter] or stuff like that then it's like shh . . . shh, but then it's like oh yeah, we have like ten students of color in the STEM majors and we are diverse so when everything is going perfectly then like we are the prize, but when other things are going on that may not be as politically acceptable, then let's sweep them under the rug, like they're not here."

As Jillian made clear, how the university took credit for the work of students of color seemed especially egregious given how communities of color were not supported. Further, how predominantly white universities celebrate the accomplishments of students of color presents a clear dilemma for those of us in higher education. While we want to recognize and celebrate these successful students, we also do not want to make them feel like they are being used as agents of recruitment who are complicit in a lie that is a false promise of diversity. This tension is exacerbated when the celebrations are coupled with university-sponsored recruitment activities, many of which are staffed by students of color volunteering or working part-time campus jobs.

Many students at North Middleton were hired as campus orientation leaders specifically to help recruit prospective students to campus. As a diversity ambassador, Jackie "appreciated the opportunity but also felt like it was all b.s." Jane agreed and explained that even these spaces were segregated: "This year being an orientation leader, this year there were more Black people but a lot of times I still felt excluded. They would have lunch and you know how you feel more comfortable around your own. So, the Black people would sit together, and the white people would sit together. And with other things, we would just group together, and the older people tried to break the boundaries, but it was already set." Jane, Jackie, and other students who did diversity work for the university believed these experiences would be "great" for their professional development, but at the same time, they also felt complicit in institutional lies. In addition, they were tired, knowing that they had to work more than their white peers to navigate white spaces and other permanent elite masculine whiteness as part of their job.

Sara Ahmed's study on diversity workers (2012) helps explain the experiences of our participants not just as students, but also as employees and volunteers. It is important that we, like Ahmed, shift the analysis of diversity to the nature of diversity workers' duties. Doing so further clarifies how the institution has not met its diversity goals and offers analysis on how it can improve its efforts (Ahmed 2012). From the perspective of women of color undergraduates, who often serve as paid and unpaid diversity workers on campus, it is clear how diversity is not a habit, not in the foreground, and not normed, because we see how these workers must strive to bring diversity into view. When explaining how diversity professionals bring attention to the issue, Ahmed makes it clear: "There is labor to attending to what recedes from view" (Ahmed 2012, 14).

To explain how universities quietly benefit from the labor of women of color undergraduate diversity workers, we employ a well-established concept in the sociological literature—emotional labor (Hochschild 1983). In recent years, the phrase "emotional labor" has entered the mainstream popular media under somewhat false pretenses. It has been widely used to explain inequalities in child-rearing in which women generally do more and men generally do less. We argue that this unequal distribution of household labor is more about gender and less about emotion, and encourage us to return to the original definition of and purpose for this renowned concept. When sociologist Arlie Russell Hochschild coined emotional labor, she explicitly drew on feminist theories of gender, Marxist critiques of capital, and Erving Goffman's sociological theories of emotion to make visible a specific kind of labor that is invisible and uncompensated yet contributes to capital.

Hochschild made clear three necessary conditions: First, workers must present inauthentic emotion as part of their jobs. This is evidenced by mandates in training materials, directives from supervisors, and cause for discipline. Second, workers must evoke emotions in others. Third, the work is not compensated and therefore contributes directly to profit. Although most research applies the notion of emotional labor to workers in industry, we are using it here to explain the experiences of women of color students that pivot this analytical lens on a potential cause of disparities. In other words, how does the same institution that is trying to help women of color students also inadvertently harm them?

Amber Jamilla Musser explains the work demands of faculty of color in higher education in terms of how emotional labor is employed in the classroom, student affairs, and administrative leadership. She observes, "When change only happens at the level of representation it highlights the commodification of minority bodies" (Musser 2015, 4). This can be explained by talking to the very people who are being used to represent the presence of diversity.

While recruiting and hiring women of color is attractive to the university, it often results in more work for the faculty members. They are asked to advise each group/initiative on campus, often represented by singular identity-based groups. Musser further explains this situation:

> This is the work a specimen performs for the university. But at what cost? Negative emotions, such as shame, disavowal, or anger, that one might experience at having an ambivalent relationship to a fraught identity category—a relationship that the university is banking on being public because of its push toward visibility—must be negotiated on one's own time. Positive emotions like pride are turned into material labor (one takes on this administrative duty, one hangs out with these students on one's own time). All of this is also on top of the general public burden placed on these identity categories through the public's (including the university's) policing of behavior and other forms of discrimination. (Musser 2015, 8)

Musser makes clear how the university earns profit from the visible (but not compensated) labor of faculty of color to sustain diversity accomplishments that must be brought into view in institutions that are otherwise saturated with whiteness. Therefore, the university's gain is twofold: First, it gets to celebrate its diversity successes and highlight people of color at the same time. Second, it does so in part through uncompensated emotional and performative labor provided by faculty of color, which contributes to overall institutional profit.

By centering the voices of women of color undergraduates at a predominantly white institution, we reveal how universities benefit repeatedly and specifically from these students' efforts without recognizing the cost to them. This is emotional labor. First, as diversity workers, women of color undergraduates must present inauthentic emotions as part of their job. They must hide their frustration, pain, embarrassment, and instead "push through." They must also appear eager for opportunities and grateful when they get them. Second, women of color undergraduates are asked in many informal and formal ways to evoke emotions in others. Certainly, as diversity ambassadors and orientation leaders, they must elicit hope and excitement in prospective students of color and their families. Last, does all this increase profit in predominantly white institutions of higher education? Yes. During the time of the study, North Middleton literally doubled in size, with a substantial increase in students, graduates, buildings, and administration. Not surprisingly, an increase in neoliberal diversity messages and rhetoric accompanied this growth. Campus materials disproportionately represented students of color and did so without institutional substance or support.

In Sum

After believing its promises of diversity, women of color undergraduates looked deeply for themselves at North Middleton. What they found instead was a composite of the somatic norm, supported by a permanence of white, masculine, elite spaces, that sometimes yielded segregation. As a result, they felt betrayed and deceived, but also inspired to make structural change. When they created this change for themselves, North Middleton turned a blind eye. Instead, the university highlighted a few success stories, which made those students who were featured feel complicit in the lie. Women of color undergraduates appreciated the formal opportunity to do diversity work. But in taking advantage of it, they also felt complicit because they knew that North Middleton had positioned itself as diversity accomplished rather than diversity aspirational (Ahmed 2012).

Predominantly white institutions of higher education become neoliberal universities when their diversity rhetoric and activities are only framed as accomplishments and as differences within normed preexisting permanent whiteness. The permanence of white, masculine, elite spaces is sustained in large part due to how diversity is framed as a "happy object," which can only occur by also masking actual persistent daily acts of systemic oppression (Ahmed 2012). When we acknowledge how neoliberalism pervades even the most well-meaning institutions of higher education, we make space to shift the narrative from intentions and outcomes to the process in between. Our question should not be about whether disparities exist.

Our question should concern the how: How are predominantly white universities—even the most well meaning of them—earning profit from diversity initiatives that do not challenge white, masculine, elite permanence, which ultimately supports white supremacist patriarchal capitalism?

What can predominantly white institutions do to better aspire to diversity, equity, and inclusion? It is important to represent the accuracy of our diversity accomplishments and ambitions, simultaneously reduce the cost, and always give credit where credit is due. Alongside feeling deceived and used, our participants felt an urgent need to advocate for themselves and for their communities by contributing to diversity work in all areas of campus life. As first made clear by women of color feminists in renowned collections like *This Bridge Called My Back* (1983), the legacy of how women of color shoulder the burden of diversity work is not new. When divisions and disparities are present, someone must be the bridge to understanding and acceptance. If no one with administrative power helps provide structural ways to reduce oppression and support equity, women of color will do so, and often in ways that are invisible.

In addition to undertaking formal diversity work at North Middleton, women of color undergraduates also bridged between communities of color and white communities to help foster community and unity on campus. They were asked to eliminate guilt and other negative feelings from their white peers, faculty, and staff. They helped white people understand diversity through disclosure of their own personal experiences, sometimes being asked to do so without warning or permission. These women of color undergraduates provided emotional labor as well as brilliant intellectual labor without recognition or compensation. This next discussion of the labor of bridging will help all predominantly white institutions of higher education better heal, repair, and be mindful of the complexities that are inherent in even the most well-meaning of intentions.

CHAPTER 3

"I Want to Say Something"

The Price of Bridging Labor

It's a Thursday afternoon, and I (Odette) am sitting in my European politics class. We are discussing England's colonial reign in South Africa and the current treatment of African refugees migrating to Europe. Going over my notes, I am feeling slightly nervous about where this dialogue will go. From past experiences in this class, I already know that the intersecting topics of race and politics often lead to tense conversations. I go into this discussion hoping my fears are unwarranted, but I know these fears are very much validated when a student, a white man student, says, "It should be illegal for African migrants to wear hijabs in Europe. What if they commit a crime, the police wouldn't be able to identify them. They could be dangerous." This comment is corroborated by another white student who says, "When coming to Europe, people need to assimilate to Western culture once they move here."

While I am not surprised by the racially charged comments of my white counterparts, I am left saddened by them. I feel a pit of anger boiling in my stomach as I prepare my rebuttal. Being one of the two Black students in this class, I feel required to respond to these comments to (a) humanize these migrants, (b) speak on the array of factors that led to their migration, and (c) educate these students about the harm associated with their observations. When it's my turn to speak, I see the same white male student smirk and scoff at my words while the professor seamlessly ignores his actions.

As you've just learned in chapter 2, when a university claims diversity but does little structurally to support it, someone must take up this invisible labor. The experience Odette shared above speaks to how women of color students, particularly Black women students, serve as "a bridge" between various identity-based groups. In the classroom, Odette could not let anti-immigration rhetoric dominate the discussion. Coming from an immigrant background, she felt the need to challenge the harmful statements of her peers and ensure that the whole class heard a perspective beyond the Eurocentric and xenophobic comments shared. As she described, she felt physical and emotional discomfort. But at the same time, Odette very much felt called to speak in defense of and on behalf of her communities. She—like many of our participants—knew this choice to educate her classmates was critical to understanding diversity, equity, and inclusion on campus. She believed it could help make change that would ultimately improve the campus experience for students of color. Odette also knew that her contributions were important knowledge that her classmates should have.

Many of our participants reported having to be the teachers and educators inside and outside the classroom. This meant these women served as a bridge between and among people of color and between people of color and white people in many ways: for the university, in the classroom, with men of color, with peers, and for faculty, staff, and administrators. This labor took care of North Middleton and was uncompensated and unrecognized. As a group, these women of color students promoted the university positively and encouraged overall civility on campus. Their labor, whether it was advocating for student of color issues or running educational events through student-led organizations, also helped to ensure a more diverse campus, which the university could then highlight in its promotion efforts. In addition, women of color students helped their communities by supporting and showing up for Black men and men of color, even though these efforts weren't always reciprocated. Through an intersectional approach, we will explain how the burden of being a bridge is socially experienced and systemically caused, contextualize this invisible labor, and examine the effects on women of color students. These women should not have been used as instruments to educate members of the university. However, they provided this education, in part because they knew it had to be done, and in part because they felt it was expected of them.

"Bridging labor," the term we have coined, explains and contextualizes the cost that women of color students must bear while attending PWIs. Neoliberal rhetoric often celebrates diversity and inclusion, but it does not address the specific needs of people of color, reduce oppression, or effectively educate and promote structural equity through an intersectional lens. It only causes further tension and harm.

North Middleton's neoliberal approaches to diversity created a vacuum that someone had to fill to support equity. Because North Middleton failed to live up to its promise of diversity, women of color students became bridges to understanding and acceptance, which helped to address structural divisions and disparities. If no one else could do it, women of color students would do the invisible work of being the bridge because they felt an urgent need to advocate for themselves and for their communities. However, there was usually no acknowledgment of the harm suffered by their minds, bodies, and spirits. The experiences of the women of color undergraduates you are reading about in this book are part of a long history offered in social justice education. Black, Latina, and Native feminist scholars have documented how women of color often serve as a bridge when it comes to issues of identity and diversity. This role can be liberating, but it also makes them uncomfortably hypervisible and invisible at the same time (Collins 2000; Moraga and Anzaldúa 1983).

Being the Bridge: The Legacy of
This Bridge Called My Back

Now in its fourth edition (2015, 2001, 1983, 1981), *This Bridge Called My Back: Writings by Radical Women of Color* is widely considered a foundational text on women of color feminism scholarship and activism that comes directly from the lived experiences of women of color. It was first initiated as a call to white middle-class women to stop exclusion in the feminist movement. Then the work quickly transformed into a tangible commitment to further feminism as understood by women of color. This dedication would simultaneously empower women of color and build a stronger feminist movement ultimately including *all* women. As Moraga writes in the first-edition preface, the purpose of *Bridge* is to provide a vision and a call to action:

> It was written for the women in it and all whose lives our lives will touch. We are a family who first only knew each other in our dreams, who have come together on these pages to make faith a reality and to bring all of our selves to bear down hard on that reality. It is about physical and psychic struggle. It is about intimacy, a desire for life between all of us, not settling for less than freedom even in the most private aspects of our lives. A total vision. For the women in this book, I will lay my body down for that vision. *This Bridge Called My Back*. (2001, 50)

As Moraga explains, this anthology was designed with three purposes in mind: (1) to serve as sustenance for the women who contributed to it, and for other women like them so that they are seen, heard, and affirmed; (2) to serve as a teacher to help all women see the differences between us in ways that consider power, privilege, and oppression, to listen to one another, to communicate with one another, and to learn from one another; and (3) to serve as a call to action and to explain the nature of that action: its import, its burden, and its effects.

Bridge is transformative for all women, of color and white, but only when we center the lives of women of color. As Moraga says, she will "lay her body down" for this bridge and stretch across it, because she knows it is necessary for her, other women of color, and social justice. *Bridge* moves us toward revolution, but only when that revolution is both personal and political. In the introduction to the first edition, Moraga and Anzaldúa make it clear that while the purpose of *Bridge* is self-preservation and self-transformation for all women, it is grounded in the knowledge that we begin with and learn from the experiences of women of color. Only then can the personal truly be political, transforming, and revolutionary.

Bridge also remains a call to action for white women, urging them to be sure that the feminist movement works away from exclusion and reaction and toward inclusion and solidarity. Before it was published as a second edition by Kitchen Table: Women of Color Press in 1983, *Bridge* was first published by a white woman collective in 1981. Moraga describes how, from the perspective of women of color, meetings with white women evoked dread when issues of race and color emerged in the conversation:

> The white women shrinking... pause awkwardly... keeping the voices breathless, the bodies taut, erect—unable to breathe deeply, to laugh, to moan in despair, to cry in regret. I cannot continue to use my body to be walked over to make a connection. Feeling every joint in my body tense this morning, used. Bridge also allows each of us to set that terror and fear of difference that lives in each of us, as Audre Lorde famously wrote.... How can we—this time—not use our bodies to be thrown over a river of tormented history to bridge the gap? Barbara says last night: "A bridge gets walked over." Yes, over, and over and over again. (2001, 46)

White women, and all women with various privileged identities, must honor and respect how women of color and those with other invisible, marginalized identities feel compelled to lie down, stretch, and ensure that identities are not blurred or blended in ways benefiting groups that are already privileged. As much as the bridge teaches and connects, all of us who benefit from it must also make space for nourishing its makers.

Bridge is more than an anthology produced by women of color. It is more than a foundational text on women of color feminism in women's and gender studies. It offers a concrete metaphor that helps explain the nature of, effects of, and importance of intersectional feminist praxis. In the first-edition preface, Moraga describes how she had been literally dreaming of a bridge for two years during the writing of the collection. She describes the bridge as a passage "through, not over, not by, not around, but through" (2001, 45). As Moraga wrote in a foreword to the second edition, "If the image of the bridge can still bind us together, I think it does so most powerfully in the words of Kate Rushkin: 'stretch or die'" (1983, 3).

We believe this sentiment captures the feelings of our participants who bridged as part of their campus experience. We hope to make visible and honor this work, but we also hope to support anyone who is doing bridging labor. Toward this end, we heed the words of Anzaldúa in her second-edition foreword: "We are learning to depend more on our sources for survival, learning not to let the weight of this burden, the bridge, break our backs" (1983, 4). As we will describe in this chapter, bridging labor serves to connect and teach. It is not without pain, but it is also liberating. It is necessary for the survival of women of color and of the feminist movement. It provides and evokes deep feeling, it offers new knowledge, and it furthers social justice.

Bridging Labor: The Go-To Person and the Fighter

Like so many women of color before them, our participants did extra invisible work to teach, connect, and support people of color on campus, many of whom were students. We analyzed the bridge as it occurred in our study as bridging labor of two types: being "the go-to person" and being "the fighter." Participants described how often they were called on as the resident experts on race, race and gender, and race, gender, and nationality. They became the go-to people for race-related and other identity-related conversations to bridge communication on campus by educating white peers, faculty, and staff.

The second bridging role that many women of color students took on was in the service of advancing communities of color, through the role of fighter. As the fighters, women of color served as leaders, speaking up about racial, gender, and other identity-based issues and rising above adversity even when afforded minimal grace and humanity for their efforts. As a Black woman, Veronica highlighted how she felt called to be a fighter during the campus Black Lives Matter protests, sharing how her labor was taken for granted by white students and professors: "What do you hope to gain by doing this protest? All my staff members are looking at me asking why are you all doing this? Other non–students of color looked at me eagerly saying they wanted to know about the protest, but I'm like you have to look at this from my perspective. Being a woman of color in America, I have been defending my identity, my community for as long as I can remember and now you want me to do it again for you after I spent all day fighting for my community when Google exists."

Veronica's white peers expected her to be a willing adviser since, as a student leader involved in the protest, she was seen as a fighter. However, Veronica was more than just an organizer. She was also a student who should have been allowed to leave her "organizer hat" at the door if she wanted. Her experience was one of many that demonstrated the expectation that women of color students would be willing and available to engage in educational dialogue about issues pertaining to communities of color at all times, with little regard to how these interactions weighed on them. This on-call nature of bridging labor was exacerbated by a campus that was predominantly white and normed white elite masculinity.

Sociologist and author Elijah Anderson categorizes white spaces as a perceptual category distinguished by the overwhelming presence of white people and the relative absence of Black people and other people of color, which requires people of color to navigate the white (and masculine elite) space as part of their existence (2022). For women of color, the assumption that they had to be available and willing to serve as a bridge was a required condition for their existence at North Middleton. They believed that this constant labor was necessary for their peers, professors, and the wider university to fully understand how racism, sexism, homophobia, and xenophobia affected their existence. These assumptions were normalized in part because they were supported by the "Black mammy" controlling image (Collins 2000).

With her concept of controlling images, Black feminist scholar Patricia Hill Collins provides a framework to understand how Black women get pigeonholed into the role of the go-to person due to societal expectations. Collins explains how controlling images "are designed to make racism, sexism, poverty, and other forms of social injustice appear to be natural, normal, and inevitable parts of everyday life" (2000, 69). These images are inextricably linked to structural discrimination because they lead to biases on an interpersonal and systemic level. As a result of the pervasiveness of mass media and social media in our lives, controlling images take on new heights in how they affect the lives of women of color. While stereotypes are sometimes true despite the harm of being unfairly applied to an entire identity-based group, controlling images are never true and are produced by dominant groups to sustain inequality.

As we conceptualized bridging labor, our research team saw how this work was bolstered by the long-enduring Black mammy controlling image. Collins (2000) describes the mammy controlling image as one that operates at the intersections of race, class, gender, and sexuality, and that emphasizes the misrepresentations of Black women as happy, subservient supporters of white, masculine, elite society. Historically, the Black mammy served as the embodiment of Black women's faithfulness and obedience to white society. It was used to justify the economic exploitation of Black women as they were relegated to domestic servitude post-abolition. Now the image manifests itself as Black women making less pay than their counterparts, working twice as hard for the same pay, or taking on the burden of emotional labor at their own expense. This emotional labor is invisible work that is done to make others happy, but there is little awareness of the burden that is associated with it.

In our study, we explored how this bridging labor was also emotional labor and had the same effects as requiring employees to do this work (Hochschild 1983). Veronica's story was just one example of the expectations placed on Black women to do this emotional labor. We found that women of color students were significantly burdened by the emotional labor of being a bridge of communication and education to further institutional diversity initiatives and goals. Within this mammy controlling image, Black women (and other women of color) are expected to complete various obligations and do unpaid diversity labor with little or no acknowledgment.

Bridging Labor: Both Hypervisible and Invisible

For college students, campus involvement and classroom relationships are two significant components that shape the overall college experience. Students learn how to lead, work effectively in groups, express themselves, and deal with conflict, along with other skill sets. However, the experiences surrounding student sports and clubs, student government, and the classroom vary depending on the intersecting identities of all students. For women of color students, their encounters inside and outside the classroom were at the intersections of multiple identities that had direct influence on their college experience. When serving as the the bridge, our participants had to navigate the relationship between being hypervisible and invisible in addition to doing emotional labor as part of serving in these roles. Women of color students at North Middleton expressed the ubiquitous sense of both hypervisibility and invisibility that was associated with their existence at the university.

Patricia Hill Collins conceptualizes the dual status of invisibility and hypervisibility as additional forms of identity-based mistreatment (2000). To push back on being put in the margins, many Black women have found ways to increase their visibility, including adopting such labels and stereotypes as being angry, aggressive, promiscuous, and loud (Collins 2000). Women of color are also punished for refusing to be discounted and demonized, and they run the risk of being stereotyped and dehumanized while simply fighting to be heard and validated. In PWIs, a women of color students' development and experiences are intertwined with social isolation and racial and gender-based intolerance due to the function of being in a white, masculine, and elite space. The challenges of navigating these spaces that result in their hypervisibility can leave them feeling invisible and resentful. The proximity to whiteness, masculinity, and elite spaces deeply affects the ways in which women of color interact with their white counterparts, which results in an unfair and unbalanced learning environment.

The challenges women of color face at North Middleton remain unrecognized because these students are rendered invisible. Women of color students face greater challenges than white women and men students of all races within predominantly white institutions because of institutional and systemic oppression and the permanence of whiteness, masculinity, and elite space. As such, these women remain severely underrepresented and invisible at these institutions. They're typically marginalized, and their voices and experiences are silenced. This made it nearly impossible for our participants to feel empowered and supported as students. Predominantly white institutions uphold white masculine hegemonic values and, in turn, subdue and disempower women of color.

Bridge work is an invisible burden that is in part caused by cultural taxation. Cultural taxation involves unique responsibilities placed on students of color due to identity-based experiences. These students are to fulfill service roles that provide racial, ethnic, and gender representation and diversity (Hirshfield and Joseph 2012). This concept is typically discussed regarding faculty of color, but it applies to women of color students as well. In white, masculine, elite spaces, women of color students are forced to behave in a way that upholds ideals of the space to the detriment of their well-being. The act of subscribing to these values is rooted in the notion that their professional and academic growth is determined by their proximity and conformity to whiteness and other hegemonic values. It is the tax these women must pay for their education. Allowing space for and honoring the diversity of perspectives that women of color students bring to the table would counter these ideologies in PWIs. Until this happens, the voices and perspectives of these women will remain marginalized, and they will face increased burnout that threatens their well-being and future success.

At PWIs, race and gender operate in a system that advances and sustains racist and sexist institutionalized practices that have severe consequences for women of color students, particularly Black women students, who are trying to be both seen and valued in these spaces. Throughout our research, many participants spoke about the ways in which their Blackness was constantly on display inside and outside the classroom while they felt constantly ignored and alienated by the whiteness surrounding them. It is this hypervisibility that propels white people to ostracize and alienate in academia when they perceive Black women to be ghetto, suspicious, or unbelonging in particular spaces. It is this hypervisibility that forces women of color to change their tone, be less direct in communication, or use inflection when they speak so as not to be perceived as angry, hostile, or sassy. These labels serve as controlling images that prevent women of color from being accurately represented and from bringing their authentic selves while attending PWIs.

This hypervisibility also leads some students to try to adopt a "race-less" persona for their survival, which is "the absence of behavioral and attitudinal characteristics related to a particular race" (Evans-Winters and Esposito 2010). In essence, if these women deny who they are and adopt the characteristics of the majority culture, they can be successful. However, the standards of success are not defined by these students, but by white dominant culture that fails to include the voices of marginalized identities. In white, masculine, elite spaces, the accomplishments of people of color are seen as extraordinary or rare, while the attainments of white individuals are categorized as normal. This logic is problematic in that it teaches women of color that to be successful, they cannot be their authentic selves. Moreover, it challenges and influences academic achievement, as it is challenging and difficult to excel in environments that fail to value every aspect of one's identity or identities. While these methods may help Black women survive the educational system, they do so by asking them to alter parts of themselves to be accepted in white, masculine, elite space.

Bridging Labor in the Classroom

As the go-to people in the classroom, our participants identified two interrelated conditions that help explain the experience of being simultaneously hypervisible and invisible: (1) the unfair expectations to be "the expert," and (2) the assumption of providing emotional and invisible labor as "a team player." Our participants felt pressured to be the experts when professors considered them the go-to people on all issues related to communities of color. For example, Veronica recalled an interaction when a professor asked her to talk about the Black Lives Matter protests that were being organized on campus. In this instance, the professor outsourced Veronica for educational purposes. Furthermore, this encounter served as an example of invisible labor imposed on Veronica. The professor took advantage of existing power dynamics between them when requesting that Veronica, a student, speak in class. Aware of the implications of this power imbalance, Veronica then believed she had to speak up when called on or she would not be seen as a team player. As a result, our participants felt used as classroom texts because they were responsible for and unfairly burdened by providing course material to their classmates.

During this classroom encounter, Veronica said she also thought she was positioned to be a token, as she was called to educate and to verify information (that was already accessible to everyone) for the benefit of her white classmates. Another research participant, Ari, described how often she was tokenized in the classroom:

> Always, it's just like, any, anytime, anything Black comes up anytime, you're token. Yes. Anytime. It doesn't matter if it's Caribbean, it doesn't matter if it's African. It doesn't matter. Anything with dark skin. They're like, right, Ari? I'm like, what? Oh, my God, that's so bad. What are you talking about? Or, like, I'm the token, I'm like, the spokesperson of like, all colored people. Right? And I'm like, I can't talk to you about African people. I've never been to Africa. I don't know. I'm like, you guys call me African American. I don't even know. My ancestors. Right, right. Yeah. If I'm American, that's it. That's all I can say. But like, that's it. I'm always the token or the spokesperson. Like, but like I said, I try not to take those situations. You know, as a negative, I'm just like, okay, you don't know any better. So let me express it. And I try, you know, that's it. I just try to educate people, whether it's a student, professor, anything. You just got to tell people.

Ari's experience in the classroom reiterates the perceived notion in white spaces that positions people of color as monoliths and as the spokespeople for all under-represented communities. She, like many other participants in our study, experienced constant and consistent tokenizing as the go-to expert on all things related to race and ethnicity. Communities of color come in various forms. We are different people with vastly different perspectives and experiences. By reducing these communities to a singular image, professors minimize their rich cultures, which further centers North Middleton as a white, masculine, elite space. Ari knew this and did the internal work to not take it "as a negative" and instead consider it an opportunity "to educate people." As a fighter, she knew "you just got to tell people."

The tokenized status of women of color students at North Middleton encouraged us to value ourselves based on what we do and what we produce rather than who we are. This concept relates to the second challenge: the idea that women of color are expected to readily engage in invisible work to be team players in service of white institutions and societies. When our white peers leaned on us for information, information that they could have easily researched themselves, we felt that burden. Jane expressed as much: "I shouldn't have to do your dirty work." Women of color students who experienced these encounters continued to be unacknowledged by the university. Either that work was ignored or it was seen as part of what a woman of color student in white spaces should just do. As a result, our participants felt required to engage in dialogue that reinforced their invisibility against the backdrop of North Middleton's elite masculine whiteness.

In serving as the bridge inside and outside the classroom at North Middleton, many women of color students found themselves feeling tokenized. They experienced hypervisibility when they were treated as tokens and used to represent diversity within the institution. In chapter 2, we discussed how North Middleton strategically marketed women of color students to promote a false sense of diversity. These individuals were main fixtures on the covers of brochures and the university website to help promote inclusion to prospective students. Paradoxically, token status resulted when these women were made to feel simultaneously hypervisible (i.e., they experienced heightened scrutiny and attention) and invisible (i.e., they experienced social isolation and lack of belonging (Moraga and Anzaldúa 1983). In other words, although frequently highlighted, our participants felt invisible because they experienced academic, social, and epistemic exclusion. Understanding the full nature of these exclusions, as we'll explore soon, not only contextualizes how women of color students are hypervisible and invisible, but also helps analyze the burden many of our participants experienced while serving as the bridge between people of color and white people.

Many of our participants endured social exclusion in the classroom. They discussed feeling isolated, ignored, and excluded in the classroom and informal settings, noting that this experience made them feel invisible and devalued. This type of exclusion simultaneously functioned as academic exclusion. For example, Lea, a Black woman, described how white students challenged her views when they pertained to race and marginalized identities, especially when she was trying to speak up and fight for her communities:

> When we are placed in groups for assignments or discussions that focus on people of color, I feel ganged up on, that my voice and perspectives are dismissed in favor of other white people in the group. Once in class, a white student told me that I was bringing down the discussion when I spoke about how people of color are treated differently in the medical field.

Similar encounters were shared by many other women of color, and they help illustrate these students' invisible status within predominantly white institutions, especially when adopting the fighter role. Lea mentioned her change in perspective upon coming to North Middleton: "[Before then,] I never felt as strongly about issues pertaining to communities of color, only because I saw for the first time what it felt like to be a real minority." For Lea, the lack of structural diversity and relative absence of people who shared her identity made her want to speak up more about issues that affected people of color. After listening for the voices of people of color and not hearing them, Lea tried to bridge communication about race in her class to add what she believed was missing from these white, masculine, elite spaces.

As part of fighting for their communities, women of color students felt compelled to teach white individuals. These women wanted to combat stereotypes about themselves and their communities, especially when professors did not correct misinformation. For example, Stephanie, a Black woman who discussed usually being quiet in conversations about race, spoke up in a course her first year:

> We had to do a presentation on an author and there were several to choose from and this one woman chose Anna Julia Cooper and we had to have a photo for the person. And her photo was of Maya Angelou. And when the photo appeared . . . I looked at the professor, I looked at her, and obviously she knew who she was, so she looked, and I looked, and I had to interject. Excuse me that is not Anna Julia Cooper . . . we don't all look alike, two totally prominent figures of different eras. I will never forget that. It was my first year in my first women's studies class and I was like is that how it is going to be? So from that, I took it upon myself to say I won't say anything unless I feel like it had to be corrected. If I hadn't said anything, would the professor have said anything to her because I don't know because it was a white professor. Would she have said anything, or would she just dock her for a grade and not tell her why? I feel like it's important for her to know it's wrong.

Just like Lea, Stephanie thought that it was important to speak up and educate her peers, to serve as a bridge between white and Black people. However, as we saw with Lea, sometimes the response from white peers was resistance. Women of color students explained to us that they felt white students would rather put their own feelings of discomfort above the lived experiences of women of color. White students avoided bringing up race or would shut down race conversations, which ultimately preserved the classroom as a white space. The white student telling Lea that she was "bringing down the discussion" illustrates how white, masculine, elite spaces characteristically center white people. White students' unwillingness or ignorance prevents them from sitting with the distress that can arise when discussing issues of race. Instead of giving space for Lea to speak about the reality of students of color at the university, her classmates chose to center themselves and other white students.

This concept of gatekeeping on knowledge also surfaces in epistemic exclusion. This particular type of exclusion refers to the devaluation of certain topics, methodologies, and types of knowledge production. Research participants discussed feeling expected to be a spokesperson within the classroom for their race, gender, or marginalized group due to the devaluing of issues pertaining to students of color. Because those topics fall outside the norm, the institution itself did not prioritize educating professors and other staff on scholarship related to them. If that wasn't the case, then the onus of bringing knowledge related to the issues and experiences of people of color inside and outside the classroom would not fall on students of color. Veronica stated,

> I feel like there's always this need especially for a student of color that is a leader. People are always pulling you in so many different directions, like they want you to speak at this panel. Today in class one of my professors was like "How would you feel about explaining to the class next session exactly what you and the organization is doing in regard to the protest." I'm just like are you kidding me. Like we have so much to do. We have so many programs, you come to learn about it if they want to.

Veronica went on to say that some professors tend to call on her or the other few women of color in the class first during discussions pertaining to race or racial stereotypes.

Our research participants have expressed feelings of isolation and alienation due to the task of representing their racial communities. Furthermore, many students have expressed skepticism about why they are placed in the forefront of racial issues. These women shared how frustrating it is when others expect them to represent their community. At the same time, women of color students have doubted whether their contributions inside the classroom are taken seriously by their peers and professors given the unchanged racial climate of North Middleton.

Women of color students said that it was normal for them to be called on to explain racial issues on campus, and that many times these interactions occurred without their consent. They believed that they were not afforded the same luxury to be students, because they had to also be educators and counselors to their white counterparts. In their role as the bridge, these women had to endure emotional labor benefiting North Middleton: they managed their own emotions while tending to the emotions of white people. In contrast, white students were not held to the same expectations. Their existence at the university was never negatively altered because of their race. In an academic setting, women of color students had different demands and expectations related to how they were allowed to show up, all of which affected the type and amount of emotional labor they had to endure. This labor had significant negative emotional and mental effects that they also had to endure.

Our participants spoke about how hard it was to engage in any sort of racial education as women of color students without overextending themselves, censoring themselves, and soothing white students' feelings about race. Jules, a Black woman, described how she felt restricted when discussing race at North Middleton, stating, "It makes me nervous to talk about it. I have to mind my Ps and Qs." When serving as the bridge, women of color students engaged in performative behavior to navigate their nervousness. This form of behavior involves suppressing emotions or reactions to meet certain societal standards or expectations of the white space. Our participants engaged in performative behavior to navigate serving as the bridge and to resist controlling images (Collins 2000). This included conforming to racialized and gendered norms defined by white members of the community.

Women of color students also had to conform to emotional norms. During racial exchanges, women of color are expected to follow "feeling rules," such as feeling irrational or wrong, and our participants believed they had to endure this conformity silently and simultaneously hide it (Moraga and Anzaldúa 1983). Dawn, a Black woman, explained how she wanted to talk about racialized content in a training at her campus job but worried about her emotional response to the material. She was one of just a handful students of color present, and she did not want her reaction to affect the message of what she wanted to say:

> So all 100 RAs [resident advisers] had to watch the movie *Crash* as part of our training and then we were expected to have conversations about it with our staff and there were some parts that showed that some people were very close minded about a lot of things, and it was making me very antsy and anxious. And we had a staff of 16. And there were four people of color. So, there were two Black women, a Black guy and Hispanic male. And so, I'm sitting next to one of my friends, one of my coworkers, and I'm just like, people are talking and I'm just very, like, my heart is racing. And I'm just like, I want to say something. But I don't know how to articulate without sounding like a crazy Black woman. And I'm just like, sitting there and my friend reaches over. Like I was getting so worked up. And I don't even know what it was that we were talking about. But so much. I just wanted to say something, but I couldn't, like I just couldn't, get it out the way I would need for it to be said for it to come across to make sense.

After relating this story to us, Dawn further explained how this and other similar interactions took a toll on her. She was burdened by the frequent demand of being the go-to expert to educate white students, especially in ways that required her to be a team player. She was also mindful of how she was perceived by others when undertaking this role, feeling powerless to step out of this dynamic.

Unfortunately, Dawn's story is common for many women of color students, as any refusal to partake in this role is mischaracterized as anger. In *This Bridge Called My Back*, author Gloria E. Anzaldúa discusses how "feeling rules" for women of color in white spaces are racialized. These women are not afforded the space to express emotions such as anger in the same capacity as their white counterparts, even when their feelings are justified (Moraga and Anzaldúa 1983).

Their perceived anger is often supported by by white society. This is used to establish power and promote privilege, leaving women of color students in a double bind: either embrace being the bridge and deal with the burden, or reject it and be labeled as angry by white people.

Bridging Labor in Campus
Involvement and Leadership

As the go-to experts, fighters, and team players, women of color students improved diversity, equity, and inclusion efforts through their involvement with campus organizations and university initiatives. In our study, most of our participants listed an array of student organizations in which they were actively involved, and their participation included having a job on campus, being a resident assistant, and serving in leadership and mentorship roles. Women who were members of multicultural student organizations were also responsible for unofficially facilitating cultural awareness events and programming for the university. Participants stated that they undertook these activities at the behest of the groups, as other students believed it was important for these women to share their culture to educate the university. Our participants also deemed this important work, but they recognized how it took them away from focusing on themselves and their individual needs. Veronica explained this dynamic:

> Um, my junior year, currently, I didn't really see the uglies of North Middleton blatantly, in my face, until this year, and it was kind of just like, I got involved with the protests [of the Black Lives Matter Movement], and what I saw more than ever before was that I have to constantly be the bridge, or I constantly explain myself, which is very annoying to me, because I hate explaining myself every day, but then for me to have to, not only explain why this is important and why this needs to be changed, but I had to explain my identity to someone, why can she say that word but I can't say that word, or why, why are you doing this, what do you guys hope to gain from this, like why are you disrupting the day like this, well, what about . . .

Veronica's experience helps us explain the nature and the effects of being the bridge. Bridging labor in student organizations includes student involvement that fosters education—for example, explaining the value of social protest to one's peers. It also includes the effort that is necessary to explain oneself in relation to social protest—for example, how Veronica said she had to explain her identity for her white peers to understand the value of the Black Lives Matter movement.

Women of color student leaders found themselves in a precarious situation where even though they were expected to be the bridge, they would receive backlash for doing the very thing they were being asked to do. If they didn't speak up, it was bad, but if they did, they experienced repercussions that put them in a double bind (Frye 1983). Student leaders felt even more compelled to teach white people, fight controlling images, and correct misinformation. Ari explained how important it was to make it comfortable for white people to ask questions without judgment: "To be a student leader, you have to be open to being uncomfortable. So, I try to look at it like I am not just a student, I am also a teacher. So, if someone has a question, I have to be open to looking at it however way they are. I can't worry about pronouns or being politically correct because not everyone has that education to be politically correct, but they still need to know. And just try to be levelheaded and attack everything with kindness."

Students are often told about the importance of getting leadership experience, but it was striking to us how many women of color in our study were student leaders or involved in a variety of organizations and clubs on campus. Our participants likely benefited from these activities, but they also had to consider extra issues related to the work of bridging. Ari explained how she must endure "being uncomfortable" sometimes, which also helped her to be "open" to a wide variety of perspectives in her involvement efforts. Navigating this landscape as a student leader was challenging for women of color, and it became another thing their white student leader peers did not have to worry about. Ari's abilities to be open, patient, and kind should be considered examples of feminist and social justice praxis, not just a burden she had to bear. These strengths could have been more visible to North Middleton too. Although women of color students had created a significant number of leadership initiatives across the university, North Middleton failed to recognize these.

For students of color, adopting a leadership role at a predominantly white institution was exhausting and demoralizing, especially when issues pertaining to race, gender, and equity were involved. Many of our participants recalled the great effort it took to make it easier for white people to speak with them about race without the fear of being judged or ostracized. These interactions with their peers created a double bind for women of color leaders when they received backlash for educating others. Leslie, an African American woman, recounted other students' retaliation against her on social media after she helped facilitate and participated in the Black Lives Matter protest on campus. She stated,

> We wanted to have the protest to take a stand and bring awareness to how people of color are treated on campus. On campus we were not seeing a lot of active

support from white students besides asking us what they could do to fix the racial issues—like it was our job to tell them. Like I was surprised but also not surprised by the response we got from other students during and after the protest. During the protest, people were laughing at us, and some Black students were called really mean names. Also, a lot of students said a lot of hateful stuff on social media [through Yik Yak]. They would call me [racial slur] and [racial slur]. The whole interaction made me mad because it made me not want to trust people. I kept thinking any of these people in my class could have made these comments and are smiling in my face like it's nothing.

Leaders of color are often caught between dueling expectations to address racism within the university, and to endure the tremendous hostility from their white peers (Moraga and Anzaldúa 1983). These women were made to feel unsafe on campus when partaking in activism and leadership activities. Not only must women of color leaders carry the burden of being a bridge, but they must also deal with overwhelming acts of harm.

To educate peers about race and racism, Jillian, a Black woman, was asked to create an informative poster that was displayed in her residence hall. She hoped that the poster would serve as a starting point for stimulating dialogues pertaining to race, diversity, equity, and inclusion. However, it was negatively received by other students and was even torn down without her consent. The backlash Jillian faced was not addressed by North Middleton. Instead of contending with the harm that Jillian encountered, the white resident adviser was more concerned about maintaining peace and decided to not find the parties responsible for demolishing her poster. These actions led to a more divided residence hall. It should have been the resident adviser, residence hall staff, and university addressing issues of race and racism to ensure North Middleton upheld its commitment to diversity on campus. Instead, that role fell to Jillian. More importantly, Jillian's harm remained unaddressed by the university, and the responsibility to create diversity again fell to a woman of color student.

Jillian's story highlights a disconnect between the predominantly white institutions that present themselves as allies for people of color and the actions these institutions consistently take to prioritize whiteness. North Middleton recognized the importance of addressing discrimination, but it was less likely to take actionable steps to advocate for and uplift people of color. In white, masculine, elite spaces, the dismissal of Black people and other people of color occurs because their status in this space is always questioned and uncertain, meaning they are held in pejorative regard by their white counterparts (Anderson 2022; Puwar 2004).

Bridging Labor in Greek Life

During the time of our study, the Office of Greek Life at North Middleton wanted to find ways to build unity between the Multicultural Greek Organizations (MGO), Interfraternity Council (IFC), and Panhellenic Council (PHC). The Greek organizations included historically Black, Latino, and other multicultural fraternities and sororities, which attracted mostly students of color, but also some white students. The IFC included historically and predominantly white fraternities at their events; these also attracted mostly white students, but also students of color. The PHC included historically and predominantly white sororities, and these, too, attracted mostly white students, as well as some students of color.

The purpose of the Office of Greek Life was to provide advice, programming, and support to all these organizations. However, our participants described how the office would ask them to bridge the gap between Multicultural Greek Organizations and the mainstream, predominantly white fraternities/sororities (IFC and PHC). The Office of Greek Life's quest for unity used an "equality" approach without understanding the dynamics between the three Greek councils and why multicultural Greek organizations struggled to get on the same level as the IFC and PHC. The Greek events on campus were "open" to everyone, but as we found with several aspects of campus life, such as housing, they tended to be very white and segregated.

When students did comply with the university's request to promote diversity, they were met with hostility from white students, which was clearly rooted in controlling images of women of color. These instances helped create a double doubt for our participants. They felt the dueling emotions of not being good enough from being told they don't belong in these white spaces, and the responsibility to create unity, a charge not placed on their white counterparts (Collins 2000).

A prime illustration of this burden was the campus-wide Greek week that happened every year in the spring. Its goal was to bring all Greek life organizations together, but as participants described, the event catered to the super white and mainstream organizations. During an interview, Allie, a biracial woman, explained the double standards placed on her sorority when its members sought to interact with other Greek organizations on campus:

> One experience we recently had was when we were paired with a predomi-
> nantly white fraternity and sorority, for homecoming and you know how you
> are paired together for the parade. Well, they had just assumed that the Black
> and Latino Greek organizations didn't want to participate in their dance at the

end [of the parade]. That happens a lot because there is so much tension in Greek life. We're not forced but it's kind of put upon us that we need to participate in the interfraternity council's thing. We are so small of a sorority that I think it should be in the middle. We only had 10 people from all the Black and Latino organizations come out for the event. They always say that the perception for so long is that we are the problem, that we are so standoffish but it's really not that. The first time I participated in Greek week, in their field day we got laughed at when doing the human pyramid because we weren't familiar with the rules. They went back to the organizers and told them that it's not a good idea for us to participate in these events if we are not going to be prepared or take it seriously.

The interaction Allie and the Black and Latino organizations had with the other (mostly white) Greek organizations further speaks to the controlling images placed on women of color and the othering caused by white, masculine, elite spaces. Allie's sorority members were perceived as "lazy" by the white Greek organizations in ways that helped to validate those groups' belief that a non-white organization does not belong in their event. These ideologies furthered the stigma that the event would be held in a lower regard due to the presence of people of color "infiltrating the white space." However, Black and Latino Greek organizations' willingness to participate in Greek week with the goal of promoting inclusion demonstrates another instance where women of color students had to extend themselves as a bridge while enduring the negative effects of cultural taxation.

The Office of Greek Life employed a neoliberal approach to "equality" by constantly pushing Multicultural Greek Organizations to participate in IFC and PHC events without understanding the extra labor that women of color students had to do, and the resources needed to take part at the same level. Participants involved in Greek life expressed to us how the staff from the Office of Greek Life would constantly ask them or expect them to partake in IFC and PHC affairs but not expect the reverse. Women of color described feeling pressured to put themselves out there to go to events where they felt uncomfortable and out of place. These students believed that the office was unfairly assuming they would bridge the gap that the office staff should have bridged as part of their paid work.

In its quest for equality, the office wanted all organizations to participate. However, it missed the mark because it didn't ask how students of color felt and what support they needed—whether women of color students were members in the MGO or members in the PHC. The problem was that the Office of Greek Life at North Middleton, however well intentioned, ended up off-loading the work of unity on students instead of meeting the needs of those students themselves.

Bridging Labor to Support Black Men and Men of Color

Women of color students served as leaders on campus to help remedy the discrimination and exclusion many students of color experienced while attending North Middleton. When compared with those of men of color, our participants expressed that the experiences and expectations for women of color students were drastically different. Women of color were not afforded the grace to be their "full selves" and faced racial and gender exclusion while participating in all types of organizations on campus (Lenzy 2019). This is in large part because general campus organizations have a singular focus of including women in these communities to promote institutional goals. Leslie described her experience with campus activities by saying, "Oftentimes, it feels like North Middleton tries to bury people of color, but it's really funny to me because we are the roots of the community. We basically built the community by ourselves and because of that the university has grown."

In their role as the bridge, women of color students also expressed feeling the burden of joining and managing student organizations that are devoted to helping communities of color. They joined these groups for community and for refuge from the white spaces they navigated on a daily basis. Instead, they often found themselves having to support men of color issues to uplift their community instead of receiving support from men of color on issues unique to women of color.

While participating in these organizations, several women stated that men of color were not interested in advocating for the same causes. In our study, we analyzed the relationship between Black women and men students with the hopes of gaining more insight into it and assessing the difference in how North Middleton addressed the discrimination that occurred between both groups. Throughout our study, several themes arose, including an unbalanced division of labor between Black men and women in social justice initiatives. This occurrence was also present in the relationship between Black women and men. It reminded some participants of an intergenerational pattern where Black women do a substantial amount of the work while Black men get the credit. One of our research participants, Dana, a Black woman, explains this phenomenon in greater detail:

> I feel like the Black women are more involved than the Black men, they are more likely to get involved and come out.... I think that boys are way more related and

want to hang out more. It kind of makes me think about how Black women have been the backbone and have done the work for so many years while the men just ride with it. You can actually see it here in the organization. . . . It makes me mad because when we were talking about what happened to Mike Brown at SCC and no one really came but when we have conversation about why Black girls are so mean they come to that. It's frustrating because when it really matters, they don't show up to things.

In their role as the fighters, Black women will often choose to advocate for their Blackness (their race over their other identities) in the effort to better the community. Historically, this has meant protecting the family and the community at large at the expense of themselves and their needs. This could be seen during the women's rights movement of the 1800s. Susan B. Anthony and Elizabeth Cady Stanton became the faces of the women's suffrage movement, while Black women like Sojourner Truth were kept in the background. Truth is now known for being an activist for women's rights and for her "Ain't I a Woman?" speech delivered at the 1851 Ohio Women's Rights Convention. The purpose of the speech was to elevate Black women at a time when women's rights were primarily focused on the needs of white women (Crawford 2018).

However, even when Black women put their race first, their contributions to fighting for their community are often overlooked. Women like Ella Baker, Fannie Lou Hamer, and Daisy Bates played major roles in helping propel the civil rights movement. They led organizations, and they were lawyers on school segregation lawsuits. All these women quietly organized and forcefully vocalized demands for equality, but all we hear about is the activism of Dr. King and Malcolm X. These women have led the global work of social and racial justice movements as nonstate actors, and the saliency of this hyperlocal work has long been overlooked by many. It has been shown that during the civil rights movement, the number of women who carried the crusade was much larger than the number of men (Crawford 2018). This phenomenon of Black women showing up in large numbers for the community was seen even in our study.

When examining the relationship between Black women and men in our study, another common theme came up: Black men never showed up for issues that affect Black women. Women of color students, particularly Black women, indicated that men of color frequently supported issues pertaining to other men of color and did not support those related to women of color. When we analyzed the membership of many of the multicultural organizations on campus, we noticed right away that there were more women members than men members. Multicultural groups at North Middleton include the Black Student Union and two other organizations that fall under it, an organization for Black men and another for Black women. The Black men's organization was designed to be a space for men of color, but, interestingly, this brother organization was dominated by Black women who supported its programs. Most people who attended the brother organization's events were Black women. However, the sister organization was not supported by Black men, even though the women wanted them to attend functions.

Black women are often overlooked in society's conversations about racism and sexism, even though they face both forms of discrimination simultaneously. Kimberlé Crenshaw calls this phenomenon "intersectional invisibility," and it explains how social movements and communities that are supposed to help Black women also contribute to their marginalization (1991). This invisibility be seen in the significant media attention given to the murder of George Floyd when compared with the scant attention given to the murder of Breonna Taylor. Within PWIs, discrimination that Black women and other women of color face is often overshadowed by or collapsed into issues that plague men.

Despite being expected to uplift their community, our participants stated that they felt overlooked for leadership positions in multicultural organizations where both men and women were members. Khadijah, a Black woman, shared an illuminating story:

> I think women going for a higher position, guys don't like that, mainly because my friends inspired me to, but they voted for a guy that was worse than me and they saw something in him, but also it was because he was a guy. In my head, I am more organized, I'm well spoken, I'm very attentive and I have all of these qualities and he was only a sophomore and he has a lot of room to grow and he displayed on the board, not being able to take certain criticisms. I was surprised when he became president, I was happy, but I was surprised. I was like, I kind of deserved that but . . . I want to be supportive. And when they explained it, they said oh we wanted you as president because we could actually see you in that spot and when you mess up we can see [participant] putting you back in your position. Why do I have to be the one who cleans up your mess? I don't have to do your dirty work. I shouldn't have to do that, especially when I've been here since my freshman year, and I know the ins and outs of everything.

Khadijah's peers did not vote for her, even though they knew she was qualified. Instead, the sophomore student was elected president because he had potential, even though he didn't have all the necessary skills. This sexism occurs within the Black community and other communities of color because men do not have to check all the boxes to get leadership roles, but women do. Moreover, Black women are denied prominent leadership roles but are expected to support their underqualified counterparts and clean up their messes if they make them, like Khadijah shared in her story. She did not get support from other Black men for her leadership even though her peers all recognized that she would have been a good fit for the position.

We explain the story Khadijah shared by using Paul Butler's concept of "Black male exceptionalism." The premise of this concept states that Black men are exceptionally burdened and discriminated against by society, more so than any other racial group (Butler 2013). Therefore, they need the most help. Butler goes on to discuss how the concept of Black male exceptionalism has gained currency both ideologically and economically, shaping the way we view social justice interventions, and the way larger society funds them. Black male exceptionalism is also observed in policy, such as the My Brother's Keeper initiative implemented during the Obama administration, or the programs to help men of color undergraduates instituted at North Middleton after a series of equity studies.

Primarily, the discrimination Black men face is seen as a unique experience. Based on patriarchal values and ignoring intersections with gender, Black male exceptionalism helps to explain why the educational achievements and issues of men are prioritized over those of Black women (Butler 2013). However, Black women and other women of color need support and opportunities too. While it is important to recognize the discrimination that directly affects Black men, it should be noted that problems arise when these men's issues are prioritized to the extent that they erase the experience of Black women and other women of color.

Khadijah's story and similar stories heard throughout our study allow us to conceptualize the landscape of Black women's and men's student involvement at North Middleton. Black women take on the role of supporting men because of the pervasiveness of Black male exceptionalism. Black men are considered by society to experience extraordinary difficulties and be invisible/hypervisible, "beaten down," and endangered, but the idea that Black men have exceptional problems discounts Black women's experiences (Butler 2013).

In addition, because men's problems in general tend to be prioritized over women's, Black men's issues are focused on more than Black women's issues. As Butler states, "The implication is that when both [Black] women and [Black] men receive the same blow, women are not hurt as much as men, or their pain is not as important" (2013, 503). Consequently, there is also no expectation for Black men to be successful, so when this occurs, the support and affirmation they receive will be much more visible. Furthermore, how patriarchal societies value masculinity causes men to operate on an individualized level, which explains why they are rewarded for minor accomplishments while women of color are consistently ignored (Butler 2013). This is because the oppression of Black men and men of color receives more visibility.

Not only are Black men not held to the same standards as Black women, but these men also uphold many of the same oppressive stigmas that allow Black women to feel unsupported and invisible on campus. This dynamic can be seen in the North Middleton Black Lives Matter protest, as Leslie explained:

> So many people . . . were involved in planning the BLM protest on campus, but you wouldn't know that from the coverage we got from the university paper. We spent a long time talking about how we wanted to advocate for ourselves and thought the protest would not only do that, but it would also be a way to show that we matter too. The plan was to have the protest originally only be on campus but that changed the day of the protest. . . . When we saw the coverage on the school paper, most of the pictures showed a lot of the men, they quoted a lot of them, and it made it look like they were the ones that organized everything. It was really annoying because a lot of the women's organizations planned everything, but the paper didn't even care about that.

Black women and other women of color are the architects of many social justice movements. Although one might think that women of color experience oppression from the dominant group, they can experience marginalization within their own communities as well. Black women's plight is decentered because we are positioned as the lowest, further adding to our invisible status (Anderson 2022). We are told to endure and uplift others while dealing with constant erasure. This erasure is socialized at a young age, as we are frequently taught by society to be the glue for the family. Our identities are positioned by proximity to men, and we are not allowed to be our "full selves," but instead our value is determined by our ability to care for others.

The erasure of Black women is further exacerbated by the controlling image of the "strong, independent Black woman," a combination of several controlling images analyzed by Patricia Hill Collins: the "Black lady," the "matriarch," and the "mammy" (2000). The emergence of the strong independent Black woman is attributed to various factors that date back to slavery. During this time, Black women were portrayed as physically and psychologically stronger than their white counterparts and equal to African American men; slave owners could therefore justify their enslavement (Collins 2000). Post-enslavement, systematic oppression against Black women has further contributed to the rise of this controlling image.

In the last two decades, a large percentage of Black homes were headed by single mothers. This is in large part due to the high incarceration rates of Black men. As a result, these women are assuming the role of primary caregiver and financial provider (Collins 2000). Positioned as the glue of the family, they are often socialized by the media, families, and the community to internalize and accept the narratives associated with being a strong, independent Black woman. One of our participants, Jules, explains that there are various obligations that come with fitting this image:

> It feels like we are always expected to be strong. It is not okay for us to show our emotions. One time in class, a student made a comment that they wouldn't want to date a Black girl because we are all ghetto and loud. That he prefers dating white women because they don't have an attitude. I'm not sure why he thought this was okay for him to say but it made me even more mad when I saw some Black guys agree with him. This just made me feel like we can't rely on Black men, they don't have our backs even though they expect us to have theirs. What happened in class just showed how we don't matter to some people.

Black women learn at an early age about the importance of working hard and placing the needs of others above their own. Some of them also learn that they cannot lean on or trust the Black men in their lives, who may believe in negative controlling images like the ones Jules mentioned in her story. Black feminist scholars have explained that these representations are used to justify the lived experience of Black women, while also limiting their ability to cultivate a holistic and positive sense of self (Collins 2000).

The strong, independent Black woman controlling image posits Black women as possessing superhero capabilities. The construction of this stigma is very diverse, with some women leaning into this assumption, some using it as a survival mechanism, and others finding empowerment through this characterization. Recent studies have revealed that there is harm associated with this controlling image that includes detriment to these women's spiritual, physical, and mental well-being (Anderson 2022). The strong, independent Black woman controlling image also consists of the emotional regulation of Black women, as they are consistently forced to navigate challenges and discrimination in silence. Their fury must be stifled to avoid being labeled as "angry Black women." In contrast, white women are often afforded the grace to express themselves as needed. Black feminist scholar Patricia Hill Collins notes that this controlling image is also used to place the responsibility on Black women for how they are treated in society, while protecting structural institutions that maintain these racial and gendered inequalities (Collins 2000).

In Sum

Women of color students bore the cost of diversity at North Middleton, and there were major effects. In this chapter, we used Black feminist theories, intersectionality, and emotional labor theory to illustrate the specific burdens women of color students experienced as the bridge of communication and education to further institutional diversity initiatives and goals. The bridge showed up in several roles: the go-to person, the fighter, the expert, and the team player. Due to the cultural taxation that was required of them to navigate these white spaces, women of color students were positioned to be unofficial diversity workers. However, when they fulfilled their role as the bridge, they also received backlash from white peers, even though this role was an expectation from others. Women of color students' emotional labor and invisible work were uncompensated and unrecognized, leaving them exhausted and frustrated. These women felt burned out and tired, and they struggled with their mental health and physical health. These additional aspects of the college experience were not ones their white peers had to deal with and navigate.

We discussed how the bridge manifested itself in several ways and in various contexts: inside and outside the classroom and in university promotion efforts with white peers, with and on behalf of men of color peers, and for faculty, staff, and administrators. As explained in *This Bridge Called My Back*, these manifestations are rooted in a historical legacy where women of color are positioned to be a bridge due to their experiences of being both hypervisible and invisible in society. We explained that the expectation for women of color students to be bridges, as well as the justification of this exploitation of these women, stems from controlling images such as the Black mammy and the strong, independent Black woman. This exploitation is the same one that has been documented in social justice struggles, notably resistance against white supremacy and the nation-state.

Women of color work hard to sustain movements, but they are often behind the scenes when men of color and white women are recognized as leaders and the faces of the movement. The other side of this coin is that the specific struggles of women of color are overshadowed by dominant representations of the experiences of white women. In addition, the specific injustices against women of color are eclipsed by representations of injustice against men of color. Instead of exploiting women of color for their work on social justice movements, white students, faculty, staff, and the university at large need to recognize this labor and understand how these women address institutional issues on campus to the detriment of their well-being.

Black and women of color feminist theoretical traditions center the knowledge gained from an insider perspective of those marginalized in a wide variety of contexts, but especially in the production of knowledge (Collins 2000; Evans, Domingue, and Mitchell 2019; hooks 1984). In chapters 4 and 5, we explain how women of color undergraduates experienced racism, sexism, homophobia, and xenophobia, as explained and interpreted by them, and how they successfully navigated college despite these burdens. Just as Black women's writing has done so for centuries, the lessons in this book from these women of color students can "restore, repair, and replace failing or unhealthy aspects of society (Evans, Domingue, and Mitchell 2019, 4). It is this very tradition that has informed the development of intersectionality. Intersectionality is not just a theory that explains experience. It is an epistemology. It changes what we know.

CHAPTER 4

"What Are You?"

The Daily Normal

There is a price to diversity that is shouldered by women of color. The permanence of elite white masculinity that students experience might have been invisible to white administrators at North Middleton, but it affected the daily realities of women of color students. For our participants, the university was never just a space or just a university—it was a white, masculine, middle-class space. There are challenges to being a woman of color student in a white, masculine, middle-class space, as these women are required to navigate the space as a condition of their existence and education (Anderson 2022; Puwar 2004). One challenge North Middleton students faced while navigating white, masculine, middle-class spaces was the burden that came from serving as a bridge between people of color and white people. The failure of the university to structurally support the diversity it claimed led to this type of invisible labor, which was invisible in part because it was not articulated as contributing to North Middleton, although it clearly helped equity goals.

The discrepancies between North Middleton's diversity efforts and the lived experiences of high-achieving women of color students pushed us to do this study. What were the everyday conditions that women of color undergraduates faced as they navigated the university? How did it feel to be the "lost Cocoa Puffs in the Cheerios," as Tina, an African American woman, articulated in chapter 2? In this chapter, we use an intersectional lens to explain how and when women of color undergraduates experienced racism, sexism, homophobia, xenophobia, and any combination of these systemic oppressions on a daily basis. We will start with Sam's story to introduce our concept of the daily normal, which helps to explain the ongoing lived experience of being dismissed, doubted, disrespected, and dehumanized by peers, faculty, staff, and other members of the campus community.

Sam's Story

I grew up in a working-class Haitian family. I was born in one of New York's five
boroughs but raised in the suburbs of Pennsylvania. As much as my parents tried
to shield me from issues of race and class to protect my innocence at a young age,
they were unable to do so. I came from a high school that was one of the largest in
my state and most diverse in our county. When it came to going to college, I was
fortunate enough to receive a full-tuition scholarship from my alma mater, a predominantly white institution. Even though I had been accepted to five universities,
there was no other choice for me once I received that scholarship because of my
economic situation. I worried about my chosen school being mostly white and had
concerns about feeling out of place. Higher education and academia were new to
me, as I was the first one in my family to attend a four-year institution. It gave me
some comfort, though, that the university appeared to be diverse, and that many
students from my high school (some of them Black) went there. So, I thought it
wouldn't be that bad, but I felt different once I arrived on campus.

I started my university experience hyperaware and unsure whether I belonged
in what immediately seemed to be a white and well-off place. The school exuded
whiteness, from the professors who mostly didn't look like me, to the classes with
few students of color, to the way I was seeing so many white people as I walked
around campus. I felt like I always needed to be on my p's and q's. I also felt uncomfortable based on my socioeconomic status. I took the bus my freshman year while
other commuters drove to campus. I was on a scholarship. Students I met came
from out of state or from school districts that were economically well off. People
had Apple laptops that I wished I could afford. I met peers who, unlike me, had no
part-time jobs and whose parents paid their tuition and housing. It just felt like a
good amount of these students were middle-class. This was not my experience, and
I felt completely out of place. Like Dana said in chapter 2, it felt like the place was
"for the white people."

Like our participants, I also had simultaneous experiences of feeling seen (uncomfortably hypervisible) and not seen (no one seeing my experiences as a Black
woman). This incident at the beginning of my freshman year has always stuck with
me as my initiation to the university. I commuted my freshman year, so I waited
for the bus stop with my Black woman friend from high school. Even though we
had different classes, we made sure to wait for each other so that we could take the
bus back home together. One day, we were just talking among ourselves when a
car slowed down as it passed us. In the car were a couple of white guys who just
laughed and pointed at us and then drove off. My friend and I were flabbergasted.
Why would they laugh at us? We didn't know them. Was it because we were Black?

Was it because we looked "poor"? Was it because they thought we were ugly or because we were dark skinned?

I initially felt ashamed, thinking that they must think that we were losers because we took public transportation instead of having a nice car like them. Reflecting on this experience now, my line of questioning in my head was certainly influenced by what felt like a white, masculine, middle-class gaze. I just kept trying to think about how these white boys must see me, and the more I thought about it, the more it made me sad. But I was resigned. This was par for the course while living as a Black woman in the United States. My friend and I just tried to brush it off and talk about other things until the bus pulled up and we went on board.

This was the first of many of my own experiences of the daily normal, a concept that we name and explain in this chapter. The phrase "the daily normal" explains how oppressive interactions between women of color college students and faculty, staff, peers, law enforcement, and the wider college-town community are simultaneously extreme and mundane. The negative experience at the bus stop seemed ordinary to me at the time. As a Black woman in the United States, I've become used to instances where people see me as "other." The incident felt like it was normal for a Black woman. I just saw it as white boys being ignorant—the usual. I was always aware of how one can be treated differently or have different access to things because of one's race/ethnicity, gender, and class. I understood survival, resilience, and managing the daily normal from watching my family deal with being Haitian in a country where they had limited economic opportunity, and that only saw them a certain way. However, taking this knowledge with me to college didn't prevent me from experiencing psychological and systemic harm.

I felt disrespected and seen as "less than" in that experience of waiting at the bus stop. Waiting at the bus stop was a thing I did every day, whether it was to travel to school or to my job back home. Waiting for the bus was mundane, but the interaction with the white students was not mundane behavior. It was a microaggression at the intersection of race and gender. The white students laughed at two Black women students at the bus stop like we weren't their peers. The white students might have perceived what they did to be harmless, but it wasn't. In that instance, by laughing at my friend and me on campus, they reinforced my feelings about who belonged on campus and who didn't. Throughout my time at my university, I sometimes had difficulty feeling like I belonged on campus. Even though I did well academically, I struggled with feeling like I wasn't more than my race and gender when navigating the campus.

At a community vigil during my senior year, I read a poem that I had written about my struggles with belonging both on and off campus, and with wrestling with the intersections of my race and gender. I shared the difficulties I experienced at the university when it came to acceptance, noting that I wasn't the only one struggling. In the student newspaper, I'm quoted as saying,

> After my first semester, I felt like I didn't belong, and there were multiple instances where I wanted to transfer out. But I was able to get support systems through family, friends, and professors on campus who cared about me, and that encouraged me to stay. But not everyone gets that experience, and not everyone stays. I think it says a lot about our campus climate. As shown in the State of the University Address and the campus climate survey results, we have issues of racism, sexism, xenophobia, and homophobia on our campus, and that needs to be acknowledged.

The Daily Normal Explained

Sam's sentiments came from her personal experience and the research we were conducting for this book at the time. Just like Sam, our participants reported being dismissed by peers and staff, being doubted by faculty and professional staff, being disrespected by peers, faculty, and staff, and being dehumanized on campus and in the neighborhood/community. For women of color students, the daily normal was not experienced in just one setting during their time at North Middleton. It encompassed interpersonal relationships, the classroom, dorm rooms, social media, the student union, and the campus and surrounding areas. Because we conceptualized the daily normal using an intersectional lens, we could explore under which conditions various identities were and were not salient.

Throughout this book, we deconstruct the narrow definition of diversity success that focuses only on quantitative data like recruitment numbers, retention numbers, and GPA comparisons without considering the emotional and physical well-being of women of color students. We constantly heard participants express feelings of isolation and physical and emotional pain throughout our study. However, that harm was rendered invisible by North Middleton's approach to assessing its diversity goals. Recruiting and graduating more women of color students did not reduce the racism, sexism, homophobia, and xenophobia that was already a part of the campus climate. These types of oppressions often played out in micro-level interactions, but some were also macro in nature.

In one way, recruitment and retention efforts made the actual campus climate invisible by emphasizing quantitative data over qualitative experience. In another way, recruitment and retention efforts created visibility for campus climate problems, which had run under the radar due to white masculine permanence. Other times, students of color took matters into their own hands, which also increased visibility. Still, in some other ways, the daily normal was invisible to many. Our hope is to shine a light on the daily normal and the harm that women of color students experienced in trying to mitigate offenses that were simultaneously mundane, extreme, and normalized—the price of pursuing education at a predominantly white institution, however well-meaning the institution is.

In contrast to the depiction of women of color as successfully completing their undergraduate degrees with no obstacles and with complete ease, our study showed that women of color students dealt with a variety of psychological and systemic experiences of being dismissed, doubted, disrespected, and dehumanized during their journeys at North Middleton. Some scholars write about these types of interactions as "microaggressions" or as "obstacles." While we think these terms capture our participants' experiences to some degree, we choose to call these interactions "the daily normal" to illustrate the constancy of this environment endured by the participants in our study. The fact that our participants' experiences were mundane did not mean that they were not harmful. Women of color had the feeling of being both hypervisible and invisible in a white, masculine, middle-class space. To say that these micro-level interactions were something different from the norm does not quite convey how these abuses were constant and relentless. These exchanges that fall under the daily normal were the norm and were the lived experiences of our participants, making their college years different from those of their peers who were white and who were men, who did not have to experience this invisible (to them) phenomenon.

If the daily normal is such a ubiquitous phenomenon among the women of color students we interviewed, then how were their experiences invisible to the well-meaning institution wanting to support them? Why are these experiences rendered invisible to white peers, well-intentioned administrators, and the like? There are a few explanations. U.K.-born and Jamaica-raised philosopher Charles Mills explains in his book *The Racial Contract* how white supremacy leads to cognitive distortion and the epistemology of ignorance (1997). White supremacy affects how one thinks and perceives the world and renders itself invisible to the very people and institutions it benefits (Mills 1997). Whiteness and other identities of privilege cultivate blind spots, even in the most well-intentioned individuals, communities, and institutions. We see this in the way white people "woke up" to the injustices happening to Black and brown folks during the uprisings in 2020.

Another explanation is that women of color are not seen as the "somatic norm" that characterizes traditional academic spaces (Puwar 2004). White middle-class men are the typical bodies that have normed the culture, organization, and values in academia, thus excluding all other bodies. Although applied to everyone, the somatic norm is at the specific intersection of race, gender, and class as the white, masculine, elite body. This body is viewed as occupying the top of the hierarchy, and as one that naturally fits in the white, masculine, elite spaces of academia. Because it is the somatic norm, this body also harbors more privilege and entitlement than all other bodies. If one does not fit the somatic norm, one feels a burden of doubt about being in the space (Puwar 2004). Because the somatic norm connects bodies to spaces, this doubt is shared by everyone who occupies the space, which then contributes to how the experiences of women of color students are not seen, believed, or taken seriously.

The invisibility of the daily normal can also be explained by the permanence of whiteness (Ahmed 2012). This social condition is manifested in everyday circumstances and regulates whiteness as the norm. These circumstances are usually assumed for and administered by white people, and then are solidified as a universally applied institutional practice. When white people think something is harmless behavior, such as a racially insensitive joke, people of color feel harm. When white people think they're being helpful, perhaps by advising a student to not pursue graduate school, they're really being hurtful. White people and institutions do not see exclusionary practices, but people of color do because they are the ones being excluded.

Being Doubted and Dismissed

As a student, you trust that your teachers, advisers, and peers will take you seriously. You are told that your professors and counselors are there to help and support you. You are in school to do the work, whether individually or in peer groups, and take advantage of your education. You have things to contribute, you're here to learn, and you hope that people will see you as a capable student just like you see yourself. However, for many of the research participants, their expectations differed from their reality. These women discussed how they often had to defend themselves or explain themselves. Some participants explicitly analyzed others' doubt in them as being informed by negative race and gender ideologies. In other words, they knew that their ability, insight, or value was questioned because of their race and gender.

Women of color students also experienced skepticism from their peers in the classroom, specifically in group settings. Many participants named how this occurred especially in the sciences. For example, Carolyn, a multiracial Black Latina woman, said, "There were just a lot of times I felt like I was doubted as a woman of color, especially in the sciences." Sara, a Liberian woman, agreed, and explained how frustrated she became when she was ignored by her classmates, even when she was the one with the correct answer:

In my zoology lab, when I first came in there, they just wouldn't listen to me. It was kind of like they all knew what they were talking about and I thought I had a lot of good points. We had to classify shells and I'm giving suggestions, and they were just not listening to me at all. It was like I just wasn't there. When my professor came out, he said we should be classifying them by weight and height, and I was like I kind of said that to you [the group] and no one said anything. The group was one Black kid and two white kids—two guys and one girl.

Sara knew exactly how the professor wanted the group to approach the assignment. However, her fellow group members ignored her because they doubted that what she would have to say would have any value. Not only do we see evidence of how Sara's peers questioned her knowledge and insight in the group, but we also see how they dismissed her because of this doubt. This feeling of being distrusted was heightened among women of color students pursuing STEM majors, where there were even fewer students of color. Because STEM has traditionally been considered a white and masculine space, students of color, especially women of color, can be seen as "infiltrating" that space and as not belonging. Sara's race and gender were particularly salient in the interaction she described, as she was seen as deviating from the norm of whiteness and masculinity that still reigns supreme in the natural sciences (Puwar 2004). People immediately try to make sense of unfamiliar Black or brown people when they enter white, masculine, middle-class spaces. They attempt to figure these individuals out and project negative narratives onto them (Anderson 2022; Puwar 2004). At North Middleton, our participants were perceived as knowing less than their counterparts who had fit the norm.

Carol, a Black woman, also discussed how she was perceived to not have any knowledge in the classroom, and how she was ignored by her white classmates, especially in group projects:

I just feel like sometimes . . . like say you have a project, working in a group or something like that. In the group, I'm seen as like the lesser. Like to an extent because say you guys are all in a group and you're all white and I'm the only Black person. They're more like okay—we'll do this, and we'll let you know. And I mean . . . I don't have a problem with it most of the time and you know it gets done but I want to have some input on it too because it's like I have good ideas. And some better ideas than what's being said. But I just feel like they feel like that I'm a slacker, I'm just here because I'm just here so they don't want to put the work on me and then I don't do it. There are Black people who, you know, live up to that stereotype. It's like you don't do the work. You're just here because you're on financial aid and stuff. But I can give as much as y'all can give but sometimes it's like, we'll do the work and then we'll let you know what to do. You know, when it's all done. I feel like you shouldn't just put me in a category of like "Oh, she's Black so she's going to be a slacker. She's not going to do the work. So, let's just do the work for her."

Carol interpreted her white classmates saying "we'll do this, and we'll let you know" as doubting her and dismissing her input and ideas. She assumed they questioned her abilities because they thought she was a "slacker" and wouldn't be as reliable, which she attributed to negative racialized stereotypes. But more than this, Carol saw how her white classmates also felt entitled to assign her work, as if she were their subordinate, when they said, "We'll do the work and then we'll let you know what to do." The experience of being doubted and dismissed affects students academically as well as psychologically. We all know that so much learning happens while planning for group projects. Students learn not only from professors but also from their peers. However, the setting of being in a white, masculine, middle-class space where "stereotypes can rule perceptions, creates a situation that can estrange the Black person" (Anderson 2022).

The Role of Controlling Images

We use sociologist and women's and gender studies scholar Patricia Hill Collins's concept of controlling images to understand how these negative perceptions of women of color college students are shaped. An intersectional concept, the controlling image is different from a stereotype. Controlling images are false representations that are constructed to sustain unequal power relations that shape how people treat Black women and other women of color, how they receive those images, and how they respond to those images (Collins 2000). They shape people's reality and how they interact with those considered "other," providing negative cultural meaning to people's identities. Controlling images also function to force what Collins calls a "binary framing of identity" (2000). In this binary framing of thinking, we see our participants relegated to the status of "other" and therefore treated as subordinates in comparison with white students.

At North Middleton, a white, masculine, middle-class space, this binary framing rules. White middle-class men are normed as dominant, and women of color are regulated and objectified as "other." This is part of a legacy of universities that were created to educate economically prosperous white men. Although North Middleton is a state-funded institution that is supposed to be accessible to individuals from various economic backgrounds, the culture and assumptions reflect middle-class ideologies. These middle-class ideologies also affect who is assumed to be part of a certain income brackets (i.e., Black students being perceived as "poor"), even if there are Black and brown students who are middle-class themselves. This is another layer of perception that affects structures, spaces, interactions, and ideologies at North Middleton, negatively influencing women of color students' educational experiences.

Part of the reason that white students stigmatized our participants is because white people associate Black and brown people with what Elijah Anderson calls the "iconic ghetto" (2022). Although the word "ghetto" is slang commonly used by people who live in and outside urban, poor, and working-class neighborhoods, it is also a negative slur used by white and wealthy people. Anderson argues that the iconic ghetto is no longer a physical space, but rather a symbol that overemphasizes danger, poor education, violence, and crime, and falsely positions all Black and brown people as "less than" everyone else. Anderson explains that although Black and brown people come from all backgrounds and socioeconomic levels, white people associate Black and brown skin with the ghetto, therefore assuming that people of color are their subordinates. As Anderson says, the iconic ghetto has become symbolic as a "natural" Black space, which then serves as a litmus test that white people and others use to negatively assess the abilities of Black and brown people. In response, Black and brown people must "dance" to prove that they are not these images being placed on them.

Even though we as women of color try to push back on them, controlling images continue to be powerful influences on how we navigate and interact with white people, men of color, and racial/ethnic groups, as well as ourselves (Collins 2000). How does that show up in a student's day-to-day life? Based on what our participants shared, their peers neither believed that they could hold their weight in group work nor valued what they had to contribute to group work. The influence of controlling images is exacerbated by the white, masculine, middle-class space. The influence of negative representations led to judgment, skepticism, and dismissal from our participants' peers. As Sara shared in her interview, when they first saw her, the members of her lab group did not listen to her and were standoffish. As the semester went on, they started to listen to her more. Perhaps over time she proved them wrong about her knowledge of the class material, and they doubted her less. As a Black woman, she was not the perceived norm of a science student (a white man), but when her classmates saw her competency on multiple occasions, they relented. However, just as other participants have expressed, Sara believed that based on her race and gender, she had to work twice as hard to be just as good as the norm. Although her peers eventually gave her some of the respect she should have received from the beginning, there was a cost to this process. The fact that Sara had to prove them wrong is evidence of "the dance," of white, masculine, middle-class space, and of controlling images.

When women of color undergraduates were doubted by their peers, faculty, and staff, they were then dismissed as unimportant. From this, we can see the relationship between being doubted and being dismissed. Yet this is not the only way that our participants were dismissed at North Middleton. Sometimes women of color undergraduates felt dismissed due to being hypervisible, and sometimes they were dismissed by not being seen at all (i.e., being invisible as a result of the permanence of whiteness and white middle-class spaces on campus). To experience the daily normal is to be both hypervisible and invisible at the same time, to simultaneously deal with the mundane and the extreme. As Audre Lorde states perfectly, "Within this country where racial difference creates a constant, if unspoken, distortion of vision, Black [and brown] women have on one hand always been highly visible, and so, on the other hand, have been rendered invisible through the depersonalization of racism" (1984, 42). In our study, dismissal appeared in several forms. Women of color students were dismissed by being ignored, by not being seen, rendered invisible often (but not always) by white peers and advisers, and by being hypervisible through the imposition of controlling images.

The Black Girl from Philly

Many participants described how they were "put in a box," judged accordingly, and then dismissed as a result. We used the concept of controlling images to help name these findings on dismissal and explain their relationship to false narratives and systemic discrimination. One dominant yet false narrative that unfolded throughout our study is the label "the Black girl from Philly." To understand the significance of this label as a controlling image, we must understand the location of North Middleton. North Middleton is situated in a wealthy county about an hour and a half away from the city of Philadelphia. For many students of varying identities who come from and live in the city, the school is in a good location, as it is close to home but far enough away. However, students of color at North Middleton come from various locations. Black women undergraduates believed that people assumed they came from Philadelphia because of their race, and thus put the label of the "the Black girl from Philly" on them.

The representation of "the Black girl from Philly" is constructed in part from the "iconic ghetto" (Anderson 2022) and manifests multiple controlling images of Black women in one. It labels Black women as loud, opinionated, "ratchet," obnoxious, sassy, ignorant, and full of attitude. "The Black girl from Philly" image says that those who fit it come from a ghetto city full of crime, poverty, and ignorant people. These women wear big earrings, tight clothes, and long weaves. As Tina explains, "A lot of people, a lot of the Black girls get a bad rep because they think that we're from Philly, and we're ignorant and we're loud. That's one thing I always get like, girl, Black girls are loud. Or they have an attitude all the time. Or they're like super sassy. And they're disrespectful. And I'm like, no, I'm not any of those things, you know, I'm a completely different thing from that. I don't identify as those things." The controlling image of "the Black girl from Philly" was a persistent ideological myth at North Middleton at the intersections of race, gender, and class, but it had actual material consequences. This representation reduced Black women students to static people instead of multifaceted and complex individuals. This fixed view of Black women students dehumanized our participants and made it easier for white peers, faculty, and staff to dismiss them.

Many of our Black participants feared being labeled with this controlling image and other ones, especially those related to sexuality at the intersections of Blackness, femininity, and lower socioeconomic class (Collins 2000). Dana explains,

> I definitely think it's a challenge [living with white roommates]. I don't want to step on people's toes. And I don't want to be like the stereotypical Black female. I wanted to be on my best behavior at all times. Like not being ratchet. Like not having guys coming in and out or you know not like twerking all over the place or you know not going out or cursing. Just kind of like, you know, just acting a fool. So, I definitely didn't want to perceive myself as that and I honestly feel like you know when people think of Black females like I kind of think that's what they think of. You know, like ratchet and ghetto. And I wasn't tryna give off that demeanor to them. So, I was definitely kinda on my Ps and Qs, and polite and trying to get to know everyone and feel everybody out. Because I didn't want anybody to judge me in that type of way, you know just because of the color of my skin.

This was the burden of being Black in white, masculine, middle-class spaces where women of color students were seen as outside the structural and somatic norm (Anderson 2022; Collins 2000; Puwar 2004). They understood that this image would affect many aspects of their college experience, and so they had no choice but to navigate it in this white, masculine, middle-class space as a condition of their education at North Middleton.

Many of our participants believed they had to watch their p's and q's to avoid harmful interactions related to controlling images. They knew they had to do "the dance" that Elijah Anderson speaks to in his research to gain acceptance and to be seen as credible (2022). Veronica said it best: "When you're not privileged, you have to be aware. You have to know everything. You have to know what to do, when to do it, what not to do, and when not to do it." Ari further explained "the dance" as a way to try to gain credibility at North Middleton:

> I feel like being born Black, you automatically have to learn how to live two lives. I have to learn how to live in that professional, white world, like, be who we want you to be. And then I have to learn how to be like, Black enough to be accepted. So, it's like, when, of course, you know, when I'm around my friends, as I speak differently, I carry myself differently. And that's because it's just natural to, but then I know what not to say, how not to carry myself when I'm not around them, or when we get into a different area or when we're on campus, for instance. So it's like, you're, you automatically learn to put a different mask on in different places, and that everyone has different masks.

"The dance" is a performance that Black people have to do in order to distance themselves from and prove wrong negative stereotypes and controlling images while in a white space (Anderson 2022). In our study, we saw how Black women self-policed because of their fear of being negatively perceived due to controlling images and other false narratives (Collins 2000). When interacting with white students at North Middleton, participants strategized to determine how much of their Blackness combined with the womanness they thought they could show in a white, masculine, middle-class space while still being perceived as credible and belonging. These women of color eased off their personality because they knew they would already be prejudged. In addition, they were careful, and they did not complain. Respectability politics, another "dance" that Black women especially must adhere to, became a tool for several participants to help mitigate the effects of controlling images rooted in the intersections of their race and gender. As Dana mentioned in her earlier quote, she made sure she stayed on her p's and q's to ensure her white roommates could not "judge [her] in that type of way" or use a controlling image to dismiss her. Some women embraced being told that they were "acting or talking white" because it meant that they were not seen as "the Black girl from Philly."

Not Being Seen

Black scholars have long discussed how Black people must "dance" in response to disingenuous questions from white people in public white spaces (e.g., "Can I help you?") as a way to flag a potentially dangerous person (Anderson 2022; Williams 1992). Participants shared stories of people either assuming their racial or ethnic identity and getting it wrong, or questioning them to figure it out. Both situations were simultaneously invasive, dismissive, and dehumanizing.

Some participants felt dismissed as part of their daily normal because they felt invisible due to consistently fielding questions and even skepticism about their racial identities. Many multiracial and biracial students repeatedly heard the question "what are you?" from white peers and other peers of color, as if their racial identity were an appropriate conversation starter. Mary, Nancy, and Naomi, who each identified as biracial (Black and white), were often assumed to be Latina. Mary and Nancy mentioned that people would just start talking to them in Spanish. However, for Naomi, a Black biracial (half-Black and half-Irish) Russian woman, the assumptions were revealed through questions: "People don't ask me much, but they do ask me 'what are you?' because some people will think I'm Hispanic, but I'm not. Because they think my hair is Hispanic because they just assume that if you're Black like you have the more stiff hair. Then people ask me if it's my real hair."

This "what are you?" experience also occurred with participants who had lighter skin tones. Talia, who is Indian, explained how people unnecessarily questioned her identity: "Somebody told me I was Middle Eastern, and um, which was fine, like I find Middle Eastern people gorgeous. But a lot of people will see me as Middle Eastern or just part Bangladeshi or from Sri Lanka. They just don't see because I guess I am lighter than most Indians. . . . I come from the north. So, like, my skin is like, lighter. So, they would always perceive me as like Sri Lankan, or like Bangladeshi or even Pakistani for that matter, but I'm like, you don't need to do this."

Because the role of race and ethnicity is so pervasive in our culture, it is understandable that people are curious, especially if someone appears racially ambiguous (Foeman and Lawton 2022). These inquiries are sometimes well meaning, but often they contribute to discomfort and dismissal, in large part due to the prevalence of controlling images and other negative ideologies. Dominant groups create and use controlling images to structure power so that subordinate groups stay subordinate, but these representations also influence how people understand the appearances of racial groups more broadly. As a binary social construct, controlling images shape perceptions of race literally into Black and white, which excludes biracial, multiracial, and light-skinned people. As a result, these individuals are under different types of scrutiny that manifest as intersections of racism, sexism, and classism, especially about beauty standards (Collins 2000).

In the examples we just shared, people took the liberty to tell Mary, Nancy, Naomi, and Talia what race/ethnicity they thought they were. Racial identity is a core identity for many. Trying to place people in a box they don't identify with is not seeing them for who they are, thus contributing to dismissal as part of the daily normal for our participants.

The "what are you?" question helps illustrate how the daily normal was both mundane and harmful to our participants. On one hand, it was asked so often that some of our participants had answers rehearsed and ready and considered the query normal and unremarkable. On the other hand, this question contributed to a long history of how white people have scrutinized people of color, which pained our participants and emboldened white permanence, patriarchy, and white supremacy at North Middleton. Biracial and lighter-skinned women were both hypervisible as objects and invisible as racialized gendered subjects.

Black women undergraduates were also both hypervisible as objects and invisible as subjects in ways that invalidated their experience. For example, some participants were explicitly told that they talked "too white" or were not "Black enough." Feelings of not being "Black enough" can arise because of the ways that dominant groups formulate controlling images to be *the* defining representations of Black women. When one doesn't fit these false narratives associated with African Americans generally and African American women in particular, then one can be seen as not "Black enough." That is deeply problematic because there is no metric for Blackness. Blackness is multifaceted, yet controlling images limit Black women and project a false reality of the world.

Many women shared stories of being told that they were not sufficiently Black and, in fact, "talked white." For example, Mary said, "I am one of the only people of color in my classes. At times, this can be hard when trying to connect with other students. Sometimes people tell me I sound white, whatever that means. I think I sound like myself, but it bothers me when people make those comments." Nancy agreed. She shared an interaction she had with a white woman friend who said, "Well you're barely Black, you don't look it, you don't act it."

A personal form of dismissal, these interactions were very frustrating to our participants and caused them pain. What did Nancy's friend mean? What did it mean to look Black and act Black? What made a white woman think she was the judge of what it means to be Black, to be a Black woman? While this white woman friend might have thought her comment was mundane and had no ill intent, it was also one that was supported by white masculine permanence at North Middleton, and it felt terribly dismissive and disrespectful to Nancy. Again, we see how women of color, specifically Black women in this case, are put in a box. Our larger society creates a constellation of controlling images that are applied to African American women. These images organize people's perception of them, which creates a checklist of how they're supposed to act, look, and speak. These checklists and checkboxes reduce women of color to objects, which bolsters people's entitlement to comment and have a say.

Patricia Hill Collins explains how controlling images have material consequences because they embolden others to make claims about people whom they actually do not know at all. For example, a white woman who does not know anything about the Black experience believed she had the authority to speak to it and dismiss Nancy's lived experience as a Black woman. This white woman friend did not view Nancy as Black because she did not fit the controlling images through which white dominant culture dictates how Black women are: loud, sassy, ghetto, etc. Because these adjectives are used to describe women of color, often Black, Latina, and multiracial women, they support controlling images that Black men and other men of color do not encounter or experience. White permanence helps explain how a white woman took it on herself to define Blackness for Nancy. She felt entitled to tell Nancy she didn't really look Black. In the process, the woman objectified Nancy by defining her based on her own standards of appearance of Blackness and femininity. This "binary framing of identity" also helps explain how the white woman friend (the subject) viewed Nancy (the object) to be appraised and assessed on her Blackness and femininity. However, how Nancy chooses to show up in the world is what it means to be a Black, biracial woman because she, and not anyone else, makes meaning of her experience as a Black person.

Being Disrespected

The third psychological and systemic facet of the daily normal is how participants were consistently disrespected by white faculty, professional staff, and their peers. Women of color students had to field stares and glares, violations of personal and bodily space, and invasive questions and statements that occurred as everyday experiences in the dorms, in classes, and in other public and private spaces on North Middleton's campus. We use an intersectional lens to analyze the conditions under which these experiences were sexist, racist, and/or xenophobic.

"The Look": Being Stared At

One prominent way that participants felt disrespected was by being stared at as they walked around campus, entered the classroom, or even took part in intimate encounters like one would have in a dorm room. They considered these stares a clear indication of people's surprise that they—as women of color—were there, and that they did not belong at North Middleton. As Jules explained, "One thing I do experience is being stared at by other students, I guess people aren't used to African American people. The feeling I get is why are they here?" Like Jules, many of our participants experienced these stares from white people and interpreted them as signs of being "other." In chapter 2 we drew on Nirmal Puwar's concept of "the look" to explain how women and people of color experience the somatic norm as they moved through spaces that were not normed for them. As Puwar states, "People are mesmerized by this object of otherness" (2004, 71). How dominant groups gaze on subordinate groups is not a neutral act; being an object of "the look" has its costs, both psychological and physical.

Kaliyah, a Black Haitian woman, described a time where she felt a white woman student staring at her in class: "Sometimes I feel like, oh, no, like, I just caught her, looking at me some type of way. And she look at nobody else like that. And I get like, why does she look at me like that. And it was a little ratchetness comes out because I get defensive. But then again, I'm like, but she looked at me some type of way. And I must offend her because I'm Black. And that says a lot in itself that I can offend you just off of my skin color."

This quote illustrates how these looks are more than a moment of discomfort for women of color students or a misunderstood gesture by white people. Kaliyah, like all our participants, was well practiced at analyzing "the look." In this case, she first observed the act and questioned its intent (i.e., "Why does she look at me like that?"). Then she recognized and processed her own defensiveness ("a little ratchetness comes out"), reexamined it ("But then again . . . she looked at me some type of way"), and ultimately saw it as racism and rejected it ("I can offend you just off of my skin color"). Because being stared at was a constant experience, our participants required extra time and effort to mitigate it. Because they were cumulative, these occurrences contributed to the daily normal, which was exhausting to process.

Dawn talked about a time when she was in her dorm room and a friend of her roommate, a white woman, was intently watching her the entire time she fixed her hair:

> I think one time I was like doing my hair like I was just like twisting my hair or something in my room and of course she probably knew no Black people in her whole life probably being this close to a Black person in the same bedroom as them right now. Like not my roommate but like her friend, right? But while I was doing my hair, she was just like literally just staring at me like, if you have a question about it, I'm totally fine with you asking, like ask me a question like, What does that do for your hair? It wasn't that I didn't like it. I think it was more funnier to me than it was upsetting just because it's unfortunate that people don't really get to be exposed to anything like that.

Sometimes, like Kaliyah, our participants experienced anger and frustration, and sometimes, like Dawn, such looks were a mild and almost humorous interaction. Either way, being stared at was a pervasive feature of the daily normal, one that required extra work of women of color students and served as evidence for the somatic norm.

The white, masculine, middle-class space at North Middleton created an atmosphere that structured identity into a binary where identities that appear "different" are hypervisible and othered (Collins 2000). This otherness led to objectification. Through objectification, one becomes depersonalized (Collins 2000). In addition, invisibility happens to women of color through depersonalization. The women of color students became objects of study for their white peers, and staring at people as if they are part of an alien species objectifies them and thus removes their personhood. That has an impact: delivering a constant reminder that you're an "other," that you're different, and that you don't belong. These experiences run counter to North Middleton's promotional materials that promise everyone is welcome and all belong.

"Don't Touch My Hair"

Participants reported several other incidents of daily normed disrespect, the kind of interactions that negated personal space and bodily integrity. But how white people, especially white women, felt free to touch Black women's hair was particularly salient. Lillian, a Black woman on a primarily white sports team, described how this typically occurred for all our Black participants: "People have come up to me, like touching my hair, like not even knowing me. My teammates when I was a freshman like my first week would ask so how does this work (while touching my hair)? And anyone with common sense would know not to do that. . . . Why do I have the sense not to do that, but you don't?" Touching someone's hair should be a well-established social error, in part because it is an intimate action, but also because it is a clear violation of personal space. Yet the way in which white women have consistently felt entitled to touch Black women's hair is well documented in academic scholarship and in popular media. This normed disrespect by white women is explained in part by looking closely at the relations between white femininity and femininity of color, which are deeply rooted in how women are positioned in relation to one another to support white supremacist, patriarchal, and colonialist notions of civility.

Ari further explained how this specific act is both disrespectful and dehumanizing: "It's hair. I swear white people think we sew our hair to our head (laughs). I don't know why we would put up with so much pain. They ask us about our hair, why it looks that way, how it feels if it is natural. I don't like that. When it is natural and they ask, it's like a slap in the face, like they think Black people can't grow out their hair." Sociologists have long established how gender is produced in interaction with others. Hegemonic masculinity is produced by, with, and for men, and femininity is similarly produced by, with, and for women (Connell 2005). Hegemonic white femininity is used to norm meanings of womanhood, especially in appearance (Cole 2009; Collins 2000). These same ideologies of white beauty and appearance have supported white supremacist framings of civility (Puwar 2004). As part of this phenomenon, white women, if left unchecked, feel entitled to access to women of color in ways that assume sameness of body and experience, but erase the agency of women of color (Moraga and Anzaldúa 1983; Puwar 2004). All these factors shape relations of power that contribute to this specific act of dehumanization.

Veronica describes white women touching the hair of Black women as a violating act. It is done without consent. She also makes it clear that this aspect of the daily normal is at the intersection of race and gender that men and white women do not have to endure:

> I like different hairstyles. I wear my natural hair mostly in the fall, it's just like it's my hair, it's a part of me. And like, I don't want your fingers in it. . . . For someone to just walk up and just assume that we're on this level, or just assume that I want your dirty fingers in my hair like, it's definitely not something, I don't feel white women think about and it's definitely something Black men don't think about. . . . And then you have white women who are like "Ah, oh, is that your hair?" Like with my hair now, I get that question all the time. It's not even just from white women or Black men, but other Black women, just, people in general are just like "Is that your real hair?" . . . Like for you to assume that because I'm a Black woman that I do weaves when I don't, that's just something that I feel is like Black men and white women don't experience, like they don't even know about that cause hair is hair. No, it's not.

The questions and comments endured by our participants were invasive, rude, and disrespectful. As students, they shouldn't have had to field questions about their hair or dodge touchy hands. Our hair is an example of how the personal is political; our hair is not just hair but is about our identity as well. In our society, there is a fascination with Black hair. A lot of that is rooted in white supremacy and Eurocentric standards of beauty in part due to controlling images and ideologies that come from the "iconic ghetto." From these influences, white people believe that Black women have fake hair or don't have any long hair. For some white students, college may be the first time they are really interacting with people of color. However, that does not mean they are entitled to Black women's bodily and personal space. The white women's intention may not be to harm, but to be curious and connect with Black women students. However, intent doesn't negate the impact. Even though the white women may be trying to educate themselves, they can still cause harm. The questioning is never innocent. Invading a person's space comes from entitled privilege and from not having to be scrutinized in a white, masculine, middle-class space.

Using an intersectional lens, we analyze how Black women had to endure having their hair touched and being asked invasive and rude questions at the merging of race and gender. These types of intimate interactions are personal, but they are also politically tied to a legacy of sexism and racism that bolsters white supremacy, patriarchy, and colonialism. There is a clear burden from having to constantly field violations of your bodily space and offensive interrogations, one that white women and men of color escape. Veronica further analyzed the situation:

> You would never think that you would be chastised by it because you are part of the majority and I'm not. So, there are lines that you can cross that I can't. . . . When you're white you never have to worry about anything because you're never going to be penalized for anything that's inappropriate. And it's just like, that's not a question that you ask white women. That's not a question you even ask Hispanic women, like I know Black women with long, beautiful, natural hair, and they're just like "Oh, is that your hair?" And to continuously hear, "Is that your hair? Is that your hair? Is that your hair? Is that your real hair? Is that your real hair? I want a weave; how can I get a weave?" Or I've even had like Hispanic women say to me, oh, do you do like, a sew-in's a type of weave that you put in your hair, "Do you do sew-ins?"

Black men and white women do not get asked these questions, as Veronica pointed out while sharing and examining her experience. This line of questioning is another aspect of the daily normal that women of color students had to deal with and mitigate while navigating the white, masculine, elite spaces at North Middleton.

Carolyn, a biracial Latina and Black woman, explained how common it was for her and other women of color to have to field questions and comments about their hair. She described an experience she had with a professor during campus orientation:

> I was an orientation leader, it was the first day, and I was handing out candy and I had this professor come to me and I don't know why he thought this was ok, you're a professor, and he comes up to me and he says, I like your hair. And at this time, I had extensions in a weave, long, loose, typical European hair, and I said, thank you. Where did you get your hair? Oh is it horsehair? And I'm like, are you kidding me? Did you just say that? And at this point, how do you approach your

professor, someone who is above you, being so insensitive, so distasteful? I don't think he noticed, he was laughing, and then he left. Literally, I sat there dumbfounded for the rest of my shift, did this guy really say this to me? So wrong.

"How do you approach your professor, someone who is above you, being so insensitive, so distasteful?" Carolyn's words make it clear that inappropriate questions and comments from faculty are especially concerning due to unequal dynamics related to status. Professors have more power than students, which would keep women of color students silent about having to endure these types of awkward and uncomfortable encounters the whole semester. This endurance requires additional energy, and the cumulative effect was exhausting for our participants.

The Saliency of Nationality

When some participants discussed disrespectful comments about their culture and accent, we learned how nationality emerged as salient in our intersectional analysis of the daily normal. Our participants experienced disrespect not only through invasions of bodily and personal space, but also through invasive and culturally ignorant comments from peers, faculty, and staff. Talia shared an interaction with a coworker who, just after meeting her, asked personal questions referencing arranged marriage:

> First. He tried to be smooth with me. He asked, "what kind of guys do you have to like, what race?" Am I into? And I was like, what? What do you mean by that? And, and of course, I understood the meaning. He was a white guy and there was a white woman sitting there too and he said "No, I was just asking her." And I was like, well, like, what did she say? So she said, my parents would kill me if I like married anybody except for a white man. I was like, okay. And then he asked me, So what's your preference? I was like, I have no preference, like the qualities that I want and there are so many that if I started like, pinpointing this should be his race, like, I would never find him. So this was definitely a rehearsed answer. And I don't need to, like have a preference in race. But then this is the other question because this is what they're getting at. Right? They have to ask about arranged marriages. So, if I say something like that, they wouldn't be able to get to that part. So, then he asked me if like, my parents wouldn't be fine with it. And this is day to day life for me.

How Talia had to manage specific comments as an everyday occurrence demonstrates how xenophobia constructed the daily normal for women of color who were international students. As in other examples from our participants, the white woman in this case did not receive the same scrutiny from the white man as Talia had. But we analyze this case at the intersection of race, gender, and nationality because this daily normal interaction was largely informed by how Talia's coworker falsely understood her experience. His misapprehension was simultaneously informed by ideologies related to gender, race, and country of origin.

Accent was another marker of nationality in the experiences of our participants. It made them feel hypervisible and on display in the classroom, but it also caused them to be silent and feel less belonging on campus. Negative perceptions related to accent contributed to how international women of color students experienced dismissal from their classmates. Ava, a Black international student, explained how she avoided classroom discussion: "Most of my classes I am the darkest one as well and I don't like talking and I went in there and I said something and in the middle of me talking—a [Black] girl stopped me and said I don't know one thing you just said your accent is so heavy. Throughout that class in the semester, I was afraid to talk. Some things you don't think about until someone else says it. I didn't want to explain because I didn't want someone else to say that stuff about me."

Many of our international participants experienced instances where their nationality was hypervisible and contributed to others' disrespect of their culture. For Talia, the invasive questioning was related to her South Asian identity, but it also clearly intersected with her gender and race. Ava, too, experienced xenophobia, which was marked by how others treated her accent. Both cases make it apparent that intersectional analyses of women of color must consider systems of oppression related to colonialism and xenophobia.

Being Dehumanized

At North Middleton, women of color students had to endure dehumanization as part of their daily normal, an additional cost they had to bear to receive their college education. The experiences of dehumanization that women of color students had on campus contrasted starkly with North Middleton's "you are welcome here" message. Our study brought to light the everyday experiences of racism, xenophobia, sexism, and homophobia that women of color dealt with. We use an intersectional lens to analyze how the dehumanizing experiences of women of color students took place. Dehumanization resulted from harassment/power-based violence, sexual assault on campus and in the community, campus social media, and violence that was further exacerbated by state agents, such as the campus police.

Harassment and Power-Based Violence

Participants described having to handle various types of harassment on campus from white people and men of color. Sometimes the persecution was racist, and sometimes it combined racist comments with sexual harassment and assault. While women of color undergraduates reported feeling dismissed by white men as potential romantic partners, white men also dehumanized these students by perpetrating catcalls and other forms of street harassment that drew on racism and sexism simultaneously. When our participants ignored catcalls, these interactions escalated to ones that were more violent. Veronica described a scenario that helps to illustrate this theme:

> I was walking into town one day with a friend (another Black woman) and a group of white guys were coming out of the bar and we were minding our own business and one guy was like oh yeah, he's into Black girls, he likes big butts too, they kept making little comments, but when we ignored them, they were like f— you. This happens all the time. I had one resident, a white guy who said yeah, I know some people aren't into Black girls, but I will say I'm down with the brown, I'm down with the swirl and I'm like, you think that's a compliment?! You think that some woman out here is like oh thank god, someone is down with the swirl, like we are not pressed, we are not worried, we do not need your love and acceptance, trust and believe.

Women of color undergraduates reported other incidents like these where white men and men of color harassed them in ways that were simultaneously sexist, racist, and specifically colorist. Leslie explained how white men and men of color consistently commented on her lighter skin tone in ways that felt objectifying because they reduced her to one body part: "They [Black and Latino men] feel like they need to get a lighter color skinned girl and then say things like, 'yo, light skin' then when I ignore them, they say 'you ugly anyway.' White guys in the bar all day say, 'I love Black women, I love Black women.' There was this one Latino guy that was like, 'what are you, what are you, your skin is so nice, I love that color.'"

Black women and other women of color are negatively impacted by standards of beauty that reduce women to objects, define their worth through appearance, and also make white European facial and body features dominant. How Leslie and other light-skinned Black and brown women are sexually/racially harassed is in part due to how their skin tone is closer to white beauty standards, and thus has more value in societies that are structured by patriarchy, capitalism, colonialism, and white supremacy. As Patricia Hill Collins notes, "Blue-eyed, blonde, thin White women could not be considered beautiful without the Other—Black women with African features of dark skin, broad noses, full lips, and kinky hair" (2000, 89). As a byproduct of white supremacy and colonialism, colorism particularly informs the standards of beauty where lightness is valued at the expense of darkness (Collins 2000). As a result, the preference for lighter-skinned women may subject them to specific harassments and abuses that could appear to be privileged attention but are forms of exoticized dehumanization.

Campus and Community Sexual Assault

Sexual harassment and other forms of power-based violence also intersect with other identity-based oppressions. Ari explained how she and her girlfriend experienced dynamics of homophobia, racism, and sexism as part of their daily normal:

> I've experienced guys trying to talk to me or my significant other. And when I tell guys I am not like that, they are like oh . . . I can make you like that. If someone tries to talk to my girlfriend, they say to me, you're not a man, what you going to do, you can't live up to her expectations then all of sudden it goes to well f— you anyway just because my girlfriend doesn't want to talk to them. From other African American men, it's not the n— word but instead it's like "ugly Black bitch," well she wasn't ugly two minutes ago when you were trying to talk to her.

Sociologists of gender emphasize how violence is the key method to asserting hegemonic masculinity, which is constructed through racism, sexism, and homophobia (Connell 2005; Pascoe 2007). Intersectional feminist scholars show how violence functions at intersections of race, gender, and other identity-based oppressions (Collins 2023; Crenshaw 1992, 1991). Our participants experienced abuse from men of all races, but it is particularly important to analyze the pain they endured from men in their same racial group.

Emasculated men of color reclaim their masculinity to reclaim power, but they do so at the expense of women. Women of color intimately understand the violence inflicted on men in their communities, and as such, they are further silenced and contribute to the silencing about the violence inflicted upon them. As Jane said, "[Rape] doesn't happen in the Black community, but women are probably afraid to speak up." It is often easier and acceptable to talk about white racist constructions of Black women's sexuality (Collins 2004). However, when it comes to analyses of sexuality that implicate Black men, it is seldom acceptable for Black women to talk about them; doing so violates norms of protecting the in-group at all costs (Collins 2000). This forces women to put their needs second. Black women can experience dehumanization at the hands of both white men and Black men. It is important for Black men to be aware of the oppression they face, but also to be aware of how they often contribute to the oppression of Black women, because "all Black girls are at risk" (Matti 2016).

Some of the experiences of extreme harassment women of color endured were in the neighborhood that surrounded North Middleton. Joya, an Afro-Caribbean woman, shared a story where she was called "an n— bitch" at a traffic light. Another participant, Leslie, described an instance where she was followed and called an animal. Our global society establishes a dichotomy of non-white subpersonhood and white personhood (Mills 1997). The two are linked, and they are defined in relation and in opposition to each other (Collins 2000; Mills 1997). This dichotomy leads to the dehumanization of women of color, where white people can feel free to demean and harass them.

Harassment on Social Media

In our study, women of color students experienced harassment online as well. Social media is a pervasive medium in all our lives, especially the lives of young people. It is also a powerful tool that universities use to promote themselves. Student life offices and student organizations use it to educate and promote their programming, and members of the wider campus community use it to connect with one another. Social media is a tool to build community and connection, but at the same time, it can be dangerous. Our participants experienced many incidents of dehumanization through online media on campus. Yik Yak, a social media platform like Twitter, was used regularly at North Middleton. Launched in 2013, it swept many college campuses during the time of this study. The problem with Yik Yak is that it is anonymous. The free app allows users within a five-mile radius to share anonymous comments with one another and upvote or downvote them. Yik Yak isn't an innocent platform, as hate speech and cyberbullying flourished on it (Franklin 2021). North Middleton was not immune.

The murder of Michael Brown in 2014 helped remove the veneer of a welcoming campus at North Middleton, which exposed its racism. Just like they did during the minority day of silence discussed in chapter 2, students organized themselves and had protests, marches, and die-ins on campus and in the neighboring community in order to, in the words of Leslie, "take a stand and bring awareness to how people of color are treated on campus." Black students and other students of color were rightfully angry. During this time of advocacy, white students laughed at them, and Yik Yak became flooded with racially inappropriate posts and slurs. Yik Yak became a place where online race- and gender-based harassment at North Middleton was emboldened. Posts such as "go back to Africa" or "Black people are monkeys" became a terribly normal part of North Middleton's culture.

Both the reactions to students of color engaging in social action and the Yik Yak posts showed how much tension there was between white students and students of color at North Middleton, and our participants were at the center. As Carol, a Black woman, explained:

> There's a lot that I see on campus. It's just like disgusting to me. Like I was more disgusted with North Middleton last year when we did the die-in. It was just really disgusting because it was on the Yik Yak thing. I will never forget that. I still have that on my phone because it's unbelievable because people would always say "Oh, go back to Africa." That's just like people who you are around every day who can't even look you in your eye who have so many mean things to say about you. And it's like you guys don't even know me and it's just like [sighs], I don't mean to get emotional about it but it's just like really frustrating. Why should I have to be around people like me to be comfortable? I should be able to be comfortable wherever I go.

Leslie agreed:

> When we were doing the protests on campus and everyone was on Yik Yak and all this stuff, that hurt me. I was like, we've come so far as a people and all we are trying to do is stand up for ourselves. Some comments made me feel scared, but most made me feel angry. Then they made me not trust anyone. I was like you could have been that person that said it. I don't want to talk to you. Don't look at me. It made me so mad. One time we were outdoors, we had all our signs and we were walking and "oh, it looks like the zoo" and "why are they outside, I thought Black people don't like the cold, why don't you go back to Africa."

Carol's and Leslie's experiences illustrate the dehumanization that women of color students endured as tensions on campus rose. Their white peers explicitly demarcated them as outside the "somatic norm" (Puwar 2004). Although some of our women of color participants knew that the university wasn't as diverse or was "for the white people," they were not prepared for the blatant harassment and racist, sexist, xenophobic, and homophobic comments that circulated on this anonymous platform. The Yik Yak incident challenged the "you are welcome here" message that North Middleton promoted across the university. Once again, women of color students were reminded of who actually was welcomed there: those who fit the somatic norm of white, masculine, middle-class spaces. The sentiments expressed through Yik Yak brought the underbelly of the institution of North Middleton to the forefront. This underbelly revealed the normed center of elite white masculinity.

As an anonymous platform, Yik Yak provided a space for white students to make posts that were extremely hateful and violent and not get caught. During our study, we also saw online harassment on social media platforms other than Yik

Yak. One of our participants had made a comment about a white woman student wearing dreads, pointing out how they were cultural appropriation. Almost immediately, our participant received a great deal of online abuse from some white students on campus whose comments included racist and sexist slurs. This extreme racial/sexual harassment directly harmed her, created a hostile climate for other Black women students, and showed how pervasive the permanence of whiteness was on North Middleton's campus.

Both examples of social media harassment demonstrate the racism and sexism that already existed at North Middleton but was not as visible to the broader community. The Yik Yak fiasco and the reaction to the post about the white woman with dreads harmed and outraged students of color. Already feeling isolated and unwelcomed, some of them started to fear coming to campus after the Yik Yak responses. Dana expressed a fear of a "mass shooting at the office of multicultural affairs." Like Leslie mentioned, Black women thought they couldn't trust anyone. Having to feel on guard constantly exacerbated what was already a daily normal of tension, disrespect, and dehumanization.

Violence by State Agents

Harassment also was exacerbated by state agents—primarily campus police, but sometimes police officers in the surrounding community. Because Black women and other women of color students were hypervisible in white, masculine, middle-class spaces, they were often targeted in ways that white students were not. This targeting occurred in the student union, in residence halls, and in the surrounding town. Dana explained how campus police were never present at events sponsored by white students:

> Literally there will be hundreds of white people at the student union at these sorority events or just any type of evening programs and public safety will be nowhere. They don't mess with them, they don't get shut down. Their parties, nothing, but as soon as the Black people have an event in the [student] union, you will see about five public safety officers. Just last year one of my orgs had a cookout and we had five police officers the whole time. Yeah, I just think it is ridiculous to be watched 24/7 when we are doing the exact same thing that white people are doing. It's like what you are really saying to us is that we are all rowdy, we are not to be trusted, and that we can't have the same fun experience that a white person can have without needing security. I think what makes it hurtful to Black people is that they are not acknowledging it, they are not trying to fix it, they are just keeping it the way it is.

The "iconic ghetto" hovered over Black and brown students at North Middleton. They could not escape being relegated to that racialized space (Anderson 2022). Even though Black and brown students were in white, masculine, middle-class spaces at North Middleton, the spaces they inhabited and congregated in became raced and gendered by white people who had projected the iconic ghetto onto them. Students of color, particularly Black students, are viewed as a threat to the somatic norm. Campus police assumed that if groups of Black and brown students came together, then there would be trouble. The controlling images of students of color, particularly Black and Latinx students, were so powerful that they influenced how campus police engaged with students of color. Dana provided additional analysis of campus police that demonstrates how the officers were an agent of dehumanization: "I think they are very rude. They look down at us ready to make any kind of move and they are going to just shut the party down. They just look at us like the first move and you're out of here and they are scowling with their eyes. It's not a friendly atmosphere. They make it very uncomfortable, and they make it known that, 'we are not here to protect you, we are here to protect the other students away from you guys.'"

Students of color are seen as infiltrating white, masculine, middle-class spaces, thus making them hypervisible and appear not to belong. Black and brown people become relegated to separate spaces since they are viewed as perpetually contaminating themselves and the space that they are in (Mills 1997). White students are seen as the status quo. The spaces they inhabit are normalized. So when white students have parties, they aren't seen as a threat—they're seen as just doing stupid college student things. One group is given the benefit of the doubt; the other group is guilty until proved innocent.

In Sum

Our women of color students were high-achieving, accomplishing many things, but at an invisible and unspoken price. In this chapter, we illustrated the cost that women of color students paid to obtain their education at a PWI. They were thriving academically but hurting socially and psychologically. Their campus experiences were shaped by various intersections of race, gender, nationality, and sexuality. Nationality and sexuality emerged as new salient data, while race and gender were deductive findings. We saw connections between all four types of the daily normal and the continuum of harm, from the mundane to the extreme. Sometimes being doubted led to dismissal or disrespect. Sometimes being dehumanized led to being dismissed or disrespected.

It is especially important to recognize the mundane factors in the daily normal, because those seemingly ordinary experiences that are normalized add up. Just because something is normalized does not make it okay. Participants reported how professors did not believe they would succeed in their degree programs, especially in the sciences. Participants reported that professors did not address microaggressions from peers that occurred in the classroom. Participants reported normalized patterns of racialized segregation in classrooms, residential housing, dining areas, and student organizations, all of which contributed to their marginalization, isolation, and stress. Some women of color students reported normalized patterns of sexual harassment and other forms of sexual misconduct from peers who were primarily men of color. They experienced dehumanizing incidents of abuse and other forms of violence on social media, on campus, and in town. These experiences of the daily normal only harmed women of color students and eroded their psychological and physical safety.

The psychological and systemic cost of being in a white, masculine, middle-class space with a lack of support took a toll on students. Women of color felt isolated, alone, and misunderstood. Some were made to feel "less than" others, some were not taken seriously, and some were just ignored. Not only did they have to deal with those issues, but they also believed they had no choice but to accept their current experience as normal and push through challenges. Women of color students just wanted to be treated fairly like their white peers; they did not want to be doubted, disrespected, dismissed, or dehumanized due to their race, gender, nationality, or sexuality. They just wanted people to understand what they were going through, and they just wanted to get through their education without having to worry about being caught in the "raindrops of racism, sexism, homophobia, and xenophobia" (Anderson 2022).

One participant observed that the experiences of the daily normal stuck with her, and that these were things that she shouldn't have had to deal with, even at such a young age. We heard women of color students express the following sentiments as their mottoes to help them push through difficulties: "Can only move on," "It happened; move on, and grow," and "We're here now." They endured these experiences for their education and for their future. Some students tried to lie low, and others didn't. Some students could no longer take the isolation, stress, and lack of belonging. There were participants who expressed wanting to leave the university or knew women of color friends had left the university because of these negative experiences. This is a double bind: either endure (stay) or confront (push back or leave). Both elicit backlash, and both reinforce existing controlling images.

Using an intersectional approach allowed us to have a more comprehensive view of the unique challenges and experiences women of color faced in white, masculine, middle-class spaces such as PWIs. These students had to navigate controlling images at the intersections of race, gender, nationality, and sexuality. White, masculine, middle-class spaces and the permanence of whiteness left women of color both hypervisible and invisible at the same time. When Dana shared her worry about being perceived as the stereotypical Black woman roommate, or as "the Black girl from Philly" controlling image that arose in the data, we saw the intersection of race, gender, and sexuality. We also saw the role of white, masculine, middle-class spaces, as all her roommates were white, and she was the only Black woman student. The controlling image of "the Black girl from Philly" shaped Dana's behavior, as she used respectability politics to control the narrative she feared her peers would have (that she was promiscuous, ratchet, loud) if she did not do "the dance." She had to mitigate the effects of the looming "iconic ghetto" that her peers most likely associated her with.

Controlling images have harmful implications for women of color students. They "other," objectify, and depersonalize them, and it is emotionally taxing. Controlling images contributed to the normalizing of dismissal, doubt, disrespect, and dehumanization of women of color students.

When we use an intersectional approach to analyze Talia's experience, we reveal another example of how the daily normal is constructed at the intersection of race, gender, and nationality. Coworkers asked Talia invasive questions about her dating life because she's South Asian. Their interrogation shows how white people's perceptions of women of color due to cultural ignorance rooted in white privilege put women of color students in a box. The coworkers assumed that Talia's parents are strict and expected an arranged marriage. South Asians are not a monolith, but Talia was reduced to a controlling image. As with the example above, controlling images contributed to the normalizing dismissal, doubt, disrespect, and dehumanization of women of color students.

We saw some of the ways that women of color students tried to negotiate and mitigate the effects of the daily normal. Some tried to be the bridge, as mentioned in chapter 3, whether in the classroom or in other spaces. Some adhered to respectability politics by being on their p's and q's to buffer the effects of the controlling images placed on them. These women wanted to help their communities by representing themselves in a positive way, and that helped them cope. In chapter 5, we explore in depth the ways that women of color successfully navigated North Middleton and the strategies that emerged as themes in the data. We'll also speak on the advice women of color in our study would give to younger women of color, as well as institutions and policymakers. As has been our goal throughout our study, this next discussion will highlight the power, agency, and resistance of women of color students.

CHAPTER 5

"Assume Whatever You Want about Me, but Let Me Blow Your Mind"

*Successes and Strategies of
Women of Color Students*

How does an act of survival become an act of thriving? In the last chapter, we shared how our participants named and explained their experiences of multiple intersecting forms of oppression. Without these words, perspectives, and analyses, this information would remain invisible and therefore could not be included in even the most well-meaning of diversity, inclusion, and equity strategies. When PWIs fail to investigate and prioritize the complexity of what it takes for women of color students to succeed, they end up taking them and their efforts for granted. As a result, these women are left to navigate false diversity promises, struggles from bridging labor, and the daily normal of multiple invisible forms of oppression. The experiences and wisdom from our participants reveal a terrible underbelly to the success of North Middleton. Yet as important as it is to reveal the hidden price of success, it is just as important to understand the strength and resilience that it takes for women of color students to prosper in predominantly white institutions of higher education.

Proving Them Wrong

In our study, we found that in addition to celebrating *that* women of color undergraduates thrived in a PWI, it was critical to explain *how* they did so. For example, part of what makes survival an act of thriving is our participants' joy and pride when they proved negative stereotypes and controlling images wrong. Jules, a Black woman, explained her enjoyment of knowing she would thrive and persevere despite all the negative perceptions about her: "I don't know how everybody else does. But with me, I think that I kind of get a kick out of it. Because it's like, you know, you stare at me, like, why am I here? And I have every right to be here just as well as you do. So I just don't even acknowledge it because it's like before, what do you even say? Like, I don't know, I just don't deal with it. And it doesn't bother me at all. Because I don't know. I mean, you can stare at me like why are you here but I'm still gonna be so it's like, see, that."

Jules's strategies for success were not isolated; we encountered these moments many times throughout our study. Lillian's example helps to illustrate the importance of emphasizing survival strategies while also making struggles and barriers from oppression visible. We asked Lillian the same questions about campus dynamics that we had asked all of our participants. She answered in part by describing an interaction with one of her peers, a white woman in her anatomy class who expressed surprise when Lillian shared that she had received a higher grade on an exam.

Lillian rightly analyzed this encounter as one that was informed by controlling images and other negative ideologies about Black women, but she did not stop there. The second part of the story, arguably the most illuminating part, is when she explained how this encounter made her feel powerful:

> Last year I took Anatomy 1 and there were probably in my lecture, maybe ten Black people and there were like 80 people in the class and it was fine, and some of the Black people were football players so they didn't really take class seriously and a lot of the people in general don't know anything else so they assume that every person of color is dumb and won't get good grades. And there was this girl that said, 'Oh how did you do, I did so poorly on the test, I got an 85.' You could tell that she just wanted attention because an 85 on an anatomy exam is great, like it's fine. And I didn't say anything because I don't like when people ask me how I did on exams especially when I know that they are just doing it to compare themselves. And she kept asking. So, I said, um . . . I got a 96. And she said you did?! And I said [louder] yeah! I did! I got a 96! [laughter] And she just shut up. And I love doing that. I love surprising people. Assume whatever you want about me but let me blow your mind. My dad told me, that is the best revenge. If you know in yourself that you are doing the best that you can and when people assume things about you, that doesn't mean that you have to do that. You do the exact opposite. And you show them that they are not the only ones that can do well. They are not the only ones that can be successful. I love it.

The sheer joy and pride that Lillian conveyed in retelling this story illustrates a couple of important points. First, her pride can be interpreted as belief in and love of self, which is a long-established strategy of self-preservation for Black women and other women of color (Evans, Domingue, and Mitchell 2019; Collins 2000). Second, how Lillian both names and explains her strategy for resistance gives voice to her own experience, but it also creates a path for other women of color to do the same. Collectively, this opposition manifests itself on an individual level and on a social level as a sisterhood between women of color. These forms of resistance also offer new truths about the student experience and new understandings of success. They serve as knowledge claims and, taken together, provide important contributions to critical social theory and other epistemologies (Collins 2000).

Black and other women of color intellectuals have long brought voice to the particular strength, power, and pride that come from resisting oppression. This is not meant to take the focus off those responsible for creating and sustaining oppression, nor is it meant to minimize the harm persecution causes. Rather, women of color scholars make visible the struggle of survival to be clear about the nature and direction of systemic harm that is done to them. This is done to call attention to how women of color maintain their sense of self within white, masculine, elite spaces. Without these assertions, racist/sexist/homophobic/classist exploitation would continue to be masked and falsely rationalized through controlling images and rhetoric (Collins 2000). In other words, the perspectives of women of color intellectuals and activists offer a corrective to explanations for inequality that are common, but also profoundly untrue.

The Personal Is Political

Many of us have likely encountered the saying "the personal is political," but what is perhaps less well known is how its genealogy is rooted in the resistance of women of color and Black feminist thought. As an analytic lens, the approach is to consider the relationship between personal experiences and political and social life. Audre Lorde teaches us that survival is not an academic skill. She emphasizes the power of personal experience in the construction of knowledge, contending that we, as feminist scholars and activists, should make this our central area of focus. There is power in illuminating the personal experiences of those who are positioned to be powerless: "It is learning how to stand alone, unpopular, and sometimes reviled, and how to make common cause with those others identified as outside the structures in order to define and seek a world in which we can all flourish. It is learning how to take our differences and make them strengths" (1984, 112).

When Lorde tells us "the master's tools will never dismantle the master's house," she reminds us that instead of seeking power from institutions or persons who already have it, or trying to fit into a society that was set up for the elite, we should harness the creative, personal voice in each of us to make a new political vision. Lorde offers another reminder: "Racism and homophobia are real conditions of all of our lives in this place and time. I urge each one of us here to reach down into that deep place of knowledge inside herself and touch the terror and loathing of any difference that lives there. See whose face it wears. Then the personal as the political can begin to illuminate all our choices" (1984, 113). She asks that each of us pause, be brave, and face our fears. She tells us to gently find our biases and be clear who is the face, the face that created the bias in the first place. If Lorde were here with us right now, we bet she would say that face is not ours, but rather that of the master—the one who benefits by trying to divide us. Rather than succumb to division, Lorde calls us to define ourselves, be courageous, be humble, and empower one another.

The phrase "the personal is political" is only useful when we consider how personal experiences are identity based. Although true, it is not sufficient to say that one's personal experience influences politics; rather, we must say how it influences politics. Black and other critical race feminisms reveal how personal experiences are shaped by multiple intersecting identities (Lorde 1984; hooks 1984). Thus we should take note from those closest to the experience about how to best achieve social justice and let them teach us. In other words, we should listen and learn.

That said, it is important, especially for those of us who are white or otherwise privileged, to avoid glorifying the strength of Black women and other women of color without also acknowledging the harm done to them (Smith and Moore 2019). Connecting the personal to the political is not just about bringing voice to our own experiences. It is also about investigating how identity informs political, economic, and social life, including any bias we may inherit from privileged identities (Combahee River Collective 1983). With this understanding, "the personal is political" is a methodology rooted in the experiences of women of color. However, combined with an intersectional lens, it helps us to see all experiences, including those that we may miss because they are outside our personal experience, and those that we fear because we inherit biases as part of our experience. For women of color, the act of claiming the specificity of their oppression is also foundational when navigating the ideology that has challenged both the sexism they encountered within their own communities,, and the racism they endured within predominantly white institutions.

In her *Black Feminist Thought: Knowledge, Consciousness, and the Politics of Empowerment* (2000), sociologist and Black feminist scholar Patricia Hill Collins explains how the intellectual contributions of Black women that have always existed were purposefully suppressed as an act of oppression. According to Collins, this constraint also sustained power among individuals who already had the most power: "Because elite white men control Western structures of knowledge validation, their interests pervade the themes, paradigms, and epistemologies of traditional scholarship. As a result, U.S. Black women's experiences as well as those of women of African descent transnationally have been routinely distorted within or excluded from what counts as knowledge" (2000, 251).

Black feminist epistemologies demonstrate how lived experience must be considered a criterion for knowledge production. In other words, when we determine what is true and what is not, actual experience matters. Not all personal lived experiences matter in the construction of knowledge, but those that are both collectively shared and interpreted as salient in relation to identity, power, and equity help us to know more about social life generally. In other words, our participants' experiences teach us about them as individuals, but the lessons did not stop there. These women also provided us with a unique account of higher education and the relationships between DEI and student success. Identity-based experiences are not just experiences, then. They are also knowledge claims, claims that can more precisely explain a wide range of phenomena.

As educational institutions frequently reproduce gender and racial hierarchies, highlighting intersectional approaches encourages social justice and disassembles structural inequalities (Ahmed 2017). Therefore, a strong case can be made for the use of intersectional analysis in understanding and giving voice to the experiences of women of color who attend PWIs. Fostering and prioritizing the academic success and well-being of women of color requires effectively dismantling various systems of inequality by understanding their functionality on both a macro level and a micro level. Adopting an intersectional analysis will allow PWIs with this lens to begin the process.

The Black feminist theoretical tradition provides a template to see the connections between naming one's experience, individual and collective resistance, and the creation of knowledge by emphasizing the power of wisdom, sisterhood, and self-love (Collins 2000; Smith and Moore 2019). Lillian's case is not just an example that illustrates the power of one's voice in resisting oppression. It also helps demonstrate how the experience of women of color undergraduates changes the parameters defining student success.

Using the traditional definition of student achievement, North Middleton administrators would say that Lillian exemplified it because she earned a very high grade on a difficult exam. She would agree with this assessment, but her definition would not stop there. For Lillian, success was not just about her performance on the test; it was also about how the interaction with her classmate made her feel. In fact, she was less excited about the grade itself than she was about how the declaration of her grade to her classmate challenged controlling images of Black women.

Lillian's experience *and* her explanation of it contribute to a reconceptualization of student success to include pride in oneself, self-love. It is within this long and rich tradition of Black and women of color feminisms that we situate and highlight the lessons that we learned from our participants. Our participants did more than survive a PWI; they thrived in it. Their voices and experiences of power, agency, and resilience demonstrate important lessons that change the very meaning of student achievement.

The Power of Knowledge

In the face of false promises, bridging labor, and the daily normal, women of color undergraduates explained how they succeeded in college by learning about, defining, and loving themselves. Their efforts to connect with and empower other women of color students, build community for themselves, and make change exemplify "the personal is political" and other established aspects of Black feminist epistemologies: knowledge as power, self-love, and sisterhood (Collins 2000). Our participants modeled how their abilities to make meaning about their lived experiences offered a pathway to self-acceptance that enabled them to connect with others, imagine new realities, and create powerful change.

Learning and creating knowledge about themselves was essential to how our participants both survived *and* thrived at North Middleton. Joya, an Afro-Caribbean woman who self-identified as international, explained how important it was for her to learn specifically what it meant to be a Black woman in the United States. She said, "And when I came here, I felt like I was no longer just a woman, I became a Black woman and I was placed into this box. It was uncomfortable for me because I wasn't used to it, but I embraced it. It made me want to learn a lot more, becoming more aware of who I was as a Black woman and all of the things that came from that. So I remember I took an Urban Geography class and it gave me some context for why systems are set up the way that they are and the foundation for prejudice."

Upon arrival in the United States, Joya noticed how people treated her differently, but she did not have the language to explain this shift. She credited the knowledge she gained in her urban geography course with helping her understand and embrace her new "box." How Joya embraced her new position in the United States demonstrates her adaptability, which took strength and an openness to new knowledge. It also illustrates the importance of intersectional analysis—in this case, the saliency of gender, race, and nationality, and how these categories shift according to time and region.

Ari, a Black woman, explained the importance of knowledge in embracing who you are. In talking about "knowing her people," she emphasized how learning about the Black community in a more formal setting helped her pause, reflect, and make choices that were best for her:

> I have to know my people. I have to know their journey. It's amazing what was hidden even from my own eyes. Even in education. I can't get mad at people who didn't know our story because I didn't know about it. You have to learn who you are because you never know where you're going until you know where you've been. Read. Learn how to control your emotions. Learn when to give power to something and when not to. Pick your fights. My life was all about adapting so I wouldn't even know what I want unless I was asked about it and had time to think about it.

Like many of our participants, Ari was so busy adapting to white, masculine, elite spaces and predominantly white communities that she barely had time to focus on what she wanted. Learning about how the Black community and other communities of color resist oppression helped her see how she could also learn to access and preserve her own personal power. This focus on Black education can also be seen as an act of self-love, because furthering her knowledge about these communities also allowed her to see her authentic self that was outside the white, masculine, elite spaces at North Middleton.

Lea, an African American woman, spoke about how she has been able to be her true self by expanding her knowledge of Black and other marginalized communities: "Double majoring in women's and gender studies has allowed me to take so many courses about Black culture. In these classes, I have gotten to learn about the struggles of our ancestors. It has helped me feel less alone. . . . Learning from authors like bell hooks has given me the tools to talk about my oppression but has also given me the tools to protect my peace. I understand that I am not the problem, like society tells me I am." Lea's story of self-discovery and love is a common theme among our participants. Black feminist scholars have long spoken about how "loving Blackness" is also an act of resistance and can be used to defy the oppositional or white gaze (hooks 1989). For Black people and others of color, learning about self-love helps to create conditions that will allow women of color to reclaim their lives.

How our participants learned about systems of power, discovered new aspects of themselves, and increased their awareness was, for many of them, a first step in surviving and thriving at North Middleton. As Mary, a biracial Black and white woman, said, "College has helped me to see a lot of situations in ways that I could not in high school. It gave me more to think about." Deepa, an Indian woman, agreed, explaining that education allowed her to see the difference between awareness and understanding: "I became aware between freshman and sophomore year in high school. I was never bullied hard core, but it was subtle, like a glare, it was not direct like you're stupid or I hate you because you're Indian, it's them ignoring you or not giving you eye contact or excluding you, being physically uncomfortable when you're not white."

Like Mary and Deepa, other women of color undergraduates described how learning more about systems of oppression helped them to process their own experiences, past and present. Dana, an African American woman, explained, "I see the patriarchy; I see the sexism. I am learning more about it, so I want to get to a point where I am becoming more aware. Not yet, but it is my goal to learn more about it and be able to acknowledge it and see it, so I am more prepared as I get older because I am Black and a female and that is what they see." Recall how a function of controlling images is falsely portraying subordinated groups as at fault for their own discrimination (Collins 2000). Dana's growing awareness of patriarchy and other identity-based systems of oppression helped her avoid blaming herself for these experiences. "Seeing the patriarchy" helps her simultaneously see herself and how others perceive her, and see that these are two separate things. Dana's new understanding of how the patriarchy shapes other people's perception of her demonstrates power that comes from lived experience and the knowledge we obtain therefrom.

Jane, a Black woman, also talked about the importance of being knowledgeable about your position in society, deeming it necessary to the growth of oneself and the ability to "talk back" to harmful messages (hooks 1989). Before learning that her personal experiences were part of a political context, Jane would simply ignore them. "Before I would brush it off, but then I didn't do anything about it," she said. She continued, "It wasn't until I educated myself and was like whoa that is a problem you cannot say something like that to me. Tell them that's not cool, you shouldn't say stuff like that." Jane's shift in perspective demonstrates how knowledge about identity-based experiences is empowering as much as it is educational.

When she explained what it meant to "be woke," Jackie, a Black woman, also emphasized the importance of language to name and confront harmful experiences:

> What it means to be woke is to be socially aware with not only yourself but with the world. Know not just the issues that your friends or family have told you. Being woke is being aware that the government and the patriarchy is feeding you lies and sleeping and taking naps is when you act like everything is fine. You could walk past the riot and say no everything is fine, ignoring, that is sleeping. Joining the riot? That is woke. Of course you want to join for the right reasons. Don't just jump in there because you think it's fun. Understand what is happening.

To Jackie, "being woke" meant having the wisdom that harmful societal messages are lies meant to keep you powerless. "Being woke" meant using this knowledge (i.e., "understand[ing] what is happening") to gain power. Our participants knew that one way to build themselves up was to discern between the lies that come from systems of oppression and the truth that comes from self-awareness and belief in oneself.

Our participants also acknowledged how they've learned about the benefits one gets from social privilege. Cindy, a Mexican Latina, knew that perceptions of her race shifted depending on the race of the people she was with. She explained how she could no longer ignore the privilege she received when others perceived her as white: "I don't want to deny it because I know that is completely ignorant for me to do. If I'm surrounded by white people, I feel so much more Latina but if I'm surrounded by people of color, I feel that much more white. I feel like it's important to recognize that too; I feel like I would be doing something wrong if I didn't. It's using that white privilege that I have if I have any, I'm using it as my megaphone."

How Cindy felt compelled to recognize the privilege she received when perceived as white can be analyzed as an ethics of caring that is key to Black feminist thought (Collins 2000). Cindy's emotional and empathetic insight into her own shifting position lent validity to the knowledge of how power functions in relation to changing perceptions of race. How she felt white with other people of color but Latina with white people is exemplary of Patricia Hill Collins's concept of the outsider within (1986). The outsider-within perspective helps to explain the specific knowledge claims that come from being simultaneously perceived as part of a subordinate group (outsider) and as part of a dominant group (insider). The insider status offers insight into the hierarchy of power and how power functions, and the outsider status offers perspectives on experiences of oppression. Combined, they offer a unique understanding of how personal identity informs political experience, and how these identities shift according to time, place, and culture (1986).

Similar to Joya, other participants offered insights into how their experiences at North Middleton were shaped in large part by changes in place and culture. After moving to the United States from India, Talia experienced life as a woman of color for the first time. In her home country she had been treated like part of "the majority." She explained,

> I never saw myself as a woman of color because I come from a country where I am the majority. In India, we never thought about these things. I don't see it as ignorance; it just didn't come up. I could never relate it to me. The first time I became aware that it happened to me was in my diversity class and one of my friends

wanted to take my interview and the professor who gave the questions—how do you feel about moving from a country where you were majority and to a country where you are minority among minority.

Talia became aware of how people at North Middleton would perceive her as a woman of color by considering how her social location changed upon moving to the United States. This new awareness helped her understand her specific positionality at North Middleton, which also helped her better mitigate the daily normal and other experiences rooted in racism, sexism, and xenophobia. Talia's story also helps clarify how knowledge comes from lived experience shaped by socially constructed identities (Collins 2000). Lived experiences informed by identities demonstrate how these identities are socially constructed and have material effects. Talia did not experience racism and sexism in India. The fact that she did in the United States is explained in part by the way meanings of socially constructed identities simultaneously stay consistent and shift over time and place.

Women of color undergraduates survived and thrived at North Middleton by drawing on the power of knowledge. Learning about themselves, their communities, and social relations of power helped to strengthen them as individuals and reduce their experiences from the daily normal. The power that came from "becoming conscious" about racism and sexism helped these students understand their experiences at North Middleton. This knowledge also helped them to reject controlling images and affirm the validity of their lived experiences and personal meanings of success. While building an awareness and language to explain identity-based oppression was sometimes difficult, it simultaneously offered our participants an awareness and a truth, ultimately paving the way to self-acceptance and self-love.

Self-Love

Self-love is not merely a celebration of self, nor is it the confidence you get from an accomplishment, such as high GPA, placement on the dean's list, or high test scores. It is cultivated internally, and, as such, it is also the kind of feeling that carries you through the tough times, when things around you fail. Like the phrase "the personal is political," the concept of self-love has been reduced and commodified. Thus we return to its root in Black feminist thought to be clear about its political and theoretical contributions to surviving oppression and thriving in spite of it (Collins 2000). Self-love is self-definition, self-valuation, and belief in oneself. As a strategy, it is a reminder to return to self when the outside world is difficult, choose your battles, set boundaries, select goals, and speak up for yourself and others.

We asked our participants how they were able to believe in themselves, especially in the face of adversity. Overwhelmingly, their responses were about self-love. We also asked the women what advice they would give to younger versions of themselves. Veronica, a Black woman, said, "I would first tell her to love herself." Leslie, an African American woman, agreed: "Don't let anyone dehumanize you. Love yourself, because they try to teach us to hate ourselves."

Other participants talked about self-love as a strategy of resistance. Dawn, a Black woman, talked about how she learned early on to love herself as a way to counter harmful beauty standards:

> It's so important to love yourself. It's so important to love you because if you can't love you then why would anyone else you know what I mean? And, it's not easy because being a Black woman and then being a fairly plump Black woman. I probably didn't always have the best self-esteem like my friends. So, to me, it's so important to love yourself and not let society standards for what beauty is be your standard for what beauty is like. I think I'm beautiful and it's so important that you think that about yourself. And just really just to go after what you want and like really work hard for it.

For Dawn, self-love frees people from internalizing harmful messages, clearing a path for thoughts and actions that help them thrive. Some of these include setting goals that will improve one's life, and others include setting boundaries to protect oneself in potentially harmful situations. Often these ideas and actions are interrelated in a variety of ways that ultimately center and preserve self.

Jillian explained how she set goals to foster self-definition: "Having a vision, a path, you want to go. Stay focused, stay focused on your schoolwork. Avoid the noise in the background and distractions." "Stay focused" and "avoid the noise" are sound pieces of advice for any college student, but for our participants, this type of self-love was also what helped them thrive as women of color students at a predominantly white university. As we spoke about in chapter 3, women of color served as the spokespeople for issues pertaining to their race or ethnic group when discussing minorities in the classroom. Serving in this role often left these students feeling burned out and disposable. Understanding this dynamic, our participants have talked about setting boundaries with others on campus to avoid feeling used and discarded by these institutions.

Sometimes women of color undergraduates manifested self-love by setting goals for their personal growth, but at other times, our participants explained that they set goals to be a model for their communities. Dana noted that striving for success was as much for other Black women, for her family, and for her community as it was for her:

I feel like I try to get more resources and people's input and try to network on campus to find different career paths. I have always set myself to be the one who is responsible and independent. I will set goals for myself and once I set one, I will strive to do it. I will find any way to make myself be a college professor and if it's hard, it's hard, I will make myself do it. That is just what I am going to do. I will not let myself down or my family down or anyone who believes in me. The support system that I have is strong enough for me to keep pushing and other Black women don't have that so if I am in a position to do it then I am going to make sure I do it for Black people so that they can see that I did do it. I have an obligation to do it for Black women but also for my family so that my brothers see a sister who is trying to do it for herself and then they will want to do it too, which I think is very important for Black men.

How Dana found purpose through hard times expands the definition of self-love to include love of community. Self-love is not just a personal act; it is also an action that is political and connected to social justice. Self-love as inspired by the success of others also redefines the traditional model of what it means to be a successful college student. Using this lens, the act of succeeding is more than attaining good grades and other individual measures of success. It is also about putting one's energies toward a broader collective aim.

Like Dana, many of our participants also had connected their own personal aspirations to helping their families and their communities. However, extending self-love to love of community required our participants to simultaneously establish boundaries. Allie, a biracial woman, explained that while many of her personal goals involved her sorority's success, she also worked to avoid losing herself. When asked what she would say to a younger version of herself, Allie recommended, "Don't overextend yourself to the point that you're always doing something for other people and not for yourself. I find myself doing that a lot, doing more for my sorority than myself and then leaving myself behind." In other words, she—like other successful women of color undergraduates—had to make helping her communities part of self-love, but then balance these efforts with a clear practice of setting boundaries in order to preserve self.

Jackie agreed that setting boundaries was an important act of self-love. One example of setting boundaries is knowing when to take action and when to avoid confrontation. The decision to not respond to oppression is not the same as accepting it, but rather a way to preserve oneself in the face of oppression. As a white, masculine, elite space saturated with white permanence, North Middleton was characterized by daily acts of racism, sexism, homophobia, and xenophobia. Jackie explained how she recognized, responded to, and survived oppression at North Middleton:

Well, sometimes it is hard to pinpoint. I don't really think about it until like, I'm laying in bed and just think about my day and like, oh, that was racism. Dammit. That was racist, just the little things oftentimes, like, even if I do see it, if it's something personal on me, I might just like shake it off or do whatever because simply I'm just like, I don't have time for this. I'm hungry. I'm gonna go eat like I don't have time to sit here and do what you got to do. But if I see it's against someone else, I'm just like, What is wrong with you? Like you can't say that. That's horrendous. There have been a couple incidents these past couple of weeks from us. Like, what is wrong with you? Like you don't say that in public. Shut up. Like the other day, I was in the car with my fraternity brothers, and they were using the phrase "that's so gay." I'm just like, I haven't heard this since high school. What are y'all doing? And I didn't really make a big deal about it. I'm just like, I had to think about who I was in the car with. And do I really want to do this today? I'm like, no, I just kind of want to get to where I'm going. So like I choose my battles. I like to choose them wisely. And I think I've been succeeding.

Jackie is an out lesbian. When she decided to focus on herself and her next destination rather than confront the homophobic words said by her friends, she was setting boundaries in ways that preserved her energy. How and when women of color undergraduates chose to avoid confrontation was an important self-love strategy that directly contributed to their success.

Preserving one's energy can also reserve the strength that is needed for getting through difficult times. Some participants developed specific strategies to thrive through the daily normal. Talia, for example, explained how she deflected intrusive questions about her culture. As an Indian woman of color, she consistently fielded queries about arranged marriage:

Okay. And then he asked me, So what's your preference? I was like, I have no preference, like the qualities that I want and the guy are so many that if I started like, pinpointing this is, this should be his race, like, I would never find him. So this was definitely a rehearsed answer. I've been like, yeah, I've been giving this answer for so long that I've chosen the best one. Because sometimes I will say something. And I feel stupid, just because I didn't want to answer the question. But I would end up like saying something really stupid by not answering the question. So I was like, I'm just gonna say, this is like a really good answer, because I really am really picky. And I don't need to, like have a preference in race.

To field constant personal questions that are also a veil for disrespect of one's culture is an aspect of the daily normal explained in chapter 4. Understandably, Talia did not like these questions and did not want to answer them. At first she ignored them, but over time she learned to expect them and came up with her strategy for success. "I have no preference," Talia's "rehearsed answer" in response to subtext about arranged marriage in Indian culture, was an example of how she set boundaries and preserved her energy and self. By being strategic with her words and with her energy, Talia successfully took her power back. This strategy is also an example of self-love as strength and resilience: Talia valued herself enough to see the issue, identify it, understand her own feelings about it, and then come up with a viable solution.

Other participants knew so clearly how a renewed focus on self can emerge from the worst places. With tears in her voice, Jules explained this feeling: "I just went through a very bad break up. And it just shook my world and it felt like the worst and after that everything went downhill for me. And I think I am just at a point where I am finding myself all over again." Ari agreed: "If it wasn't for my professors, I wouldn't have made Dean's List because I tried to do it myself and it was too much for me. But being broken, I had to rebuild myself and actually find out who I was, and you know, take that journey." Both Jules and Ari were able to name and explain how their success happened in part because they framed struggle as an opportunity to reconnect with and renew themselves.

Self-love as a strategy for success also builds resilience that is important in times of personal and political struggle. Sometimes our participants preserved their energy. As Jules said, "A lot of times it's harder to not react. If it's nonsense, it doesn't deserve my energy at all. It's not worth the time." At the same time, self-love means standing up for yourself and encouraging others to do the same. Many of our participants advised their mentees to do this. Cindy explained how she encouraged her mentee:

> I think something I told her is that she doesn't have to take shit from people and she told me that some boys in her school are annoying and say terrible things and I told her tell them stop, don't take that. And this is something that we don't really want to do, we are told as women that it is a bad idea, that bad things will come from it, that we shouldn't, I think especially women of color are expected to stay on the sidelines, more than white women, I see that as someone who passes as white that I am not as expected to do that.

Here again, Cindy offers an example of the ethics of caring that comes from Black feminist thought (Collins 2000). She recognizes how her mentee, as a darker-skinned woman of color, is expected to be silent in ways that she, who is often perceived white, is not. Cindy's knowledge of how power functions in relation to shifting perceptions of race enabled her to take action on behalf of her mentee by encouraging her to claim her voice and stand up for herself. Standing up for oneself is an act of self-love that comes from dialogue with other women of color (Collins 2000).

Kaliyah, a Haitian woman, also described how she drew inspiration from "being the change" for others in her life—in this case, the children she works with—in ways that pushed through her own fear of speaking her mind in white, masculine, elite spaces. She said, "It's up to me to get over the fact that I might not be comfortable. That's up to me to get over that. I feel like when I allow that to stop me from speaking up I am not creating that change I want to see so I am telling these kids that you got to be the change you want to see. I tell them you can be anything but for me to say that to them it is kind of me being a hypocrite if I am in the classroom not talking because I am afraid of how I am going to be viewed, so that is up to me to get over that." Like Cindy and many other women of color students, Kaliyah found strength for herself through the advice that she had given others. This specific act of self-love is exemplary of how belief in yourself comes through struggle, but it also comes through dialogue with other women of color (Collins 2000).

In this interview, Christa—as another woman of color—affirmed Kaliyah's statements and told her, "The things you have to say are valuable, the things you want to teach those kids, you have to teach yourself. So remember that." How Christa shifted Kaliyah's focus, which had been on her students, back to a focus on self-love demonstrates the type of empowerment that results from dialogue with other women of color. A particular type of power and knowledge comes from dialogue between two subjects who are agents rather than objects (Collins 2000; hooks 1989).

Women of Color Sisterhood

Community with other women of color is the third strategy our participants identified as necessary to their successes in college. Many stated that they liked having friends from other groups, but that they needed other women of color to be able to relate to and understand their experiences at North Middleton. For example, Cindy said, "[It is important to] surround myself with people who think like me, who are liberal minded like in my major." When we asked women of color undergraduates what advice they would give to younger women, their current mentees, or even a younger version of themselves at North Middleton, they would almost always suggest seeking other women of color and spaces that were designed just for them. Some of our participants knew that they were part of a long-standing tradition that demonstrates how women of color scholars and activists have always created safe and affirming spaces for themselves. These spaces made by and for women of color illustrate the power that comes from collectives. These dialogues are also natural outgrowths of knowledge about oneself and self-love.

As a biracial woman, Mary did not feel supported by women, even other women of color, before she participated in our mentorship program: "I've never felt particularly supported by women, let alone a group of women of color, not before now. I never fit in before. I guess I wasn't Black enough." As a Black woman, Ari completely understood Mary's sentiments and believed that even spaces designed for women did not quite fit her either. She said, "We need a safe zone and people were like, 'you could go to the women's center' but I didn't always feel welcome at the women's center. It was weird to ask for help because I am so taught to be on my own." How Ari did not feel welcome at the campus Women's Center is illustrative of how feminist spaces and movements are historically and traditionally saturated in whiteness and, as such, become exclusive spaces that center elite white women's experiences (Beck 2021; Kendall 2020).

The whitening of feminism was not unique to the North Middleton Women's Center. Although the phrase "white feminism" in social media suggests it is a recent phenomenon, the history of mainstream feminism makes clear how feminism had been shaped explicitly by and for wealthy white women. It was then reserved for white elite spaces to be marketed to only those who seek the same rights as the wealthy white men in their lives (Beck 2021). When Audre Lorde instructs us that "the master's tools will never dismantle the master's house," she doesn't just remind us to be skeptical of societies that are only built for the elite; she also tells us "that this fact is only threatening to those women who still define the master's house as their only source of support" (1984, 111). In other words, the fact that "the master's tools will never dismantle the master's house" is only scary to those of us who still believe our only power comes from the master.

In an attempt to garner widespread support for women to gain the right to vote, an image of "equal rights" was issued primarily by white elite suffragettes. It was remarkably similar to images of what was considered to be the proper, or "true," womanhood of the time: soft, naturally feminine, nonthreatening, and white (Beck 2021). The centering of white wealth as the "true" image of feminism set the stage for a century of emphasis on the rights of white, cisgender, straight wealthy women against the exclusion of all others. This is not to say that feminism was just for elite women, but to be clear how and when it was constructed with only white women in mind and then appropriated to support white supremacy, capitalism, and patriarchy.

This image of feminists as white, traditionally feminine, and nonthreatening didn't just support elite white women. It also reinforced the dominance of white femininity as proper womanhood, a womanhood that is naturally fragile and in need of assistance, and, moreover, supports hegemonic patriarchal white supremacy. This portrayal of white womanhood as in need of backing is in direct opposition to the constructed representations of Black women as strong, independent, and therefore not deserving of support (Kendall 2020). When Ari said she was always taught to be on her own, it is also in part due to how society falsely frames those who are deserving of help as white, and those who are not as people of color (Kendall 2020).

Given that mainstream feminism has generally centered straight, white, middle-class, cisgender femininities, it is not surprising that women of color undergraduates have mixed feelings on the topic. Several participants named inspiration specifically from womanism, which is rooted in the experiences and knowledge of Black women. For example, Jane explicitly identified as a womanist: "I looked into feminism, but I appreciate womanism much more because I feel like mainstream feminism leaves women of color out." However, many claimed that as they learned more about feminism from critical race and intersectional perspectives, they realized that feminism wasn't just about "men versus women," but was in fact about connecting with and supporting one another—as women of color. As Jane said, "At the end of the day we are all going through the same thing. We all look out for each other."

For Tessa, an African American woman, building a sisterhood with other women of color helped her to gain the confidence to ascend to a leadership position, and to facilitate social justice and equality programs for minority communities. She explained,

> I came to the university as a transfer student and had such a difficult time making friends and fitting in being "the new girl." After a hard first semester on campus, I decided to join [one of the Black women's organizations] on campus. In doing so, I was so welcomed by everyone. It felt like a warm hug that I didn't even know I needed. Being in this group gave me a sense of community. As things started happening on campus, our group really tried to spread awareness about what was happening to Black people. . . . As I became more aware of how Black people and other people of color were treated, I really wanted to do more. This was one of the reasons why we started the town hall meetings on campus. It was weird for me because this is not something I would have done and was really scared to create this program and if it wasn't for the other women in my group, I don't think I would have done so.

Participating in a group of like-minded women helped to fill a gap for Tessa. Not only did these women serve as a strong positive presence for her, but they also afforded her the opportunity to show up as her authentic self within the group.

Veronica also explained to us the importance of finding and then connecting with other women of color students at North Middleton in ways that explicitly helped her to succeed:

> I would say a lot of it is community with other women of color who are experiencing the same thing, what is it around the kitchen table. (Where do you find other women of color?) Yeah, funny, you find them at programs here. There was this program topic about, "why do Black men hate Black women." And then there's the girl in the back of the room who's laying down the law, dropping theories left and right and you're just like [excitedly] "Oh my god! I need to be friends with you!" and then they hear you say something and then at the end of the meeting, they come up and you start talking and then her friend is going to dinner tomorrow and then you see her out and then you guys start talking and then like it just builds off the relationships you had when you first got here and off the people you meet through the people that you trust with these conversations and then that's when like you have a mirror going, and then it's like, oh yeah, I know I can talk about this with these women because they understand.

Veronica's "mirror" "around the kitchen table" directly references the very first press that was founded and directed by women of color lesbians, Kitchen Table: Women of Color Press. Today the press is renowned as a catalyst for Black feminist theory, women of color feminism, and intersectionality. But at the time, Kitchen Table: Women of Color Press was a small group of women of color lesbians who had created a place to publish their work. Cofounder Barbara Smith describes the beginnings of the press this way: "In October 1980, Audre Lorde said to me during a phone conversation, 'We really need to do something about publishing'" (1989). In addition, Smith explains the motivation for starting a press run by and for women of color: "As feminist and lesbian of color writers, we knew that we had no options for getting published, except at the mercy or whim of others, whether in the context of alternative or commercial publishing, since both are white dominated" (B. Smith 1989).

The impact of Kitchen Table: Women of Color Press was profound. While it is perhaps most known for proving that books by women of color would sell to academic and general readers, it also changed women's and gender studies, other academic disciplines, and feminist movements broadly. Works that we have referenced in this book, like *This Bridge Called My Back*, are now considered canonical in many disciplines devoted to diversity, equity, and inclusion. These works and the group of women who published them didn't just offer new writings, they produced social change. Kitchen Table: Women of Color Press literally changed the way we all considered and worked for social justice.

Being the Change You Want to See

Women of color undergraduates contributed to the legacy of Kitchen Table: Women of Color Press, Combahee River Collective, and other Black and women of color feminist organizations to create social justice as a way to thrive at North Middleton. Their use of knowledge to build self-love and then foster it through community with other women of color helped to formalize self-love as a practice informed by lived experience. Women of color undergraduates broadened their self-esteem through community and dialogue with one another, which ultimately helped to change the culture at North Middleton in ways that improved diversity, equity, and inclusion.

Jackie explained how her knowledge of both oppressed and privileged identities strengthened a popular diversity program at North Middleton:

> So just the little things. People don't think outside the box. I remember I did a program the other day. I'm out here speaking on behalf of the queer community. The leader split the room, privilege, and no privilege. I stood on the privileged side, and I felt like people were like, "what are you doing?" And I'm like, "Well, as a woman of color, I don't have any privilege. But as a cisgender, individual, I have lots of privilege and stuff that we don't even think about." I told the whole room that before I had learned nothing about trans life, but then I was like, "Oh, my God, I don't have to think about going to the bathroom. I don't have to think about who's gonna be in there, and probably out to get me. I don't have to have a second thought if I want to put on makeup or do whatever." And just to see people's faces light up and go, oh, my God, I'm just like, yeah, you never thought about that. Did you? So it's just like, it's cool that things like this happened to me.

Jackie's description of her experience at one of North Middleton's most popular diversity programs makes clear how self-love and self-definition come from sharing knowledge from lived experience. Her pride in herself is evident when she says how "cool" it was that she was able to make these points about privilege to her peers. Her contributions should also be interpreted as knowledge claims, information that helped her succeed daily, but also helped the university create inclusive and socially just education. Jackie further explained how she used her awareness of social justice to create moments of change with her friends: "Being aware is stressful because of course being woke you see everything, but it also helps, especially because now I can assist people when I see certain things happening like with relationships that I see my friends are in. If I notice that my friends are being controlling, I can say, 'Whoa that is not ok. That is sexist that you say they can't do this but you are doing whatever you want to do, that is just not fair.'" How Jackie keeps her friends in check about relationship power dynamics is an equity strategy that is rarely captured in university reports, but it is still an effective change technique that assists women of color and he university.

Many of our participants talked about wanting to be a voice for other women of color. Joya told us she took a job as a residence adviser (RA) because she believed that no person deserves to feel the way she did as an international student. "How can I be a voice for them?" she asked. Like Joya, other women of color undergraduates saw the importance of "being there" for women of color students new to the university. Many identified mentoring others to bring visibility to the accomplishments of women of color broadly. Allie explained how mentoring younger women of color would simultaneously offer her a chance to highlight these women's achievements while helping others attain them as well:

> I would love to be a mentor to a younger woman of color because I am very proud of what I have accomplished and the changes I have made on this campus for women of color, within Greek life and within classes. As cliche as it sounds and it is sad that we have to say this but really just be the change you want to see. If you want women of color to be known for all of the great things they are doing and why they are great, then you have to put in work to make it happen. If you put in this work and it is going to pay off. I have been here for almost four years and when I first started, I never thought I would be this person. You're going to come here and do what you set out to do and then you're going to do other great things on the way.

When Allie says "be the change you want to see," she knows that part of her success is to make change for other women of color on campus. She also knows that her accomplishments will inspire other women of color to continue these legacies of social justice education (Evans et al. 2019).

Jane also advised her mentees to "look out for yourself and other women of color." She explained that she didn't explicitly refer to North Middleton as a PWI or "push her views" on on these students, but she helped to cultivate conversations so that "they find their own way." Jane explained how much time she spends with her mentees to let them lead the conversation and come to their own strategies and solutions:

> I push for my mentees to be involved. Get involved, stay busy, give yourself a reason to come back. We have programs, important conversations. I don't want to be somebody that just comes and be like oh this is too much, I want to leave. I want to be part of the change. When the Black Friday Coalition went to the president, we had a list of demands, and I don't want to start that and just stop. I want to

make sure that I am one of those people who tries to make change for people after me. I am hoping that my mentees won't have to go through some of the same stuff that I had to go through, that they don't have to see some of the same stuff I had to see. I am trying to make that change for them. And then they become mentors and they can make that change for their mentees. That's the plan.

As a mentor, Jane skillfully managed her own emotions about North Middleton to help younger students navigate the university as a white space, but in doing so, she also fueled her own self-definition, self-value, and self-love. Her desire to be "part of the change" and "be one of those people who tries to make change for people after me" is right in line with the long legacy of social justice education, activism, and knowledge created by Black women and other women of color (Collins 2000).

In Sum

Rather than succumb to division, Audre Lorde calls us to define ourselves, be courageous, be humble, and empower one another (1984). Women of color undergraduates consistently demonstrated several legacies of Black women and other women of color in education: the power of knowledge, self-love, communities created for and by women of color, and creating change. Using a Black feminist epistemological framework, we do not analyze these themes separately, instead explaining them as interconnected and constantly informing one another. Women of color undergraduates use a combination of these strategies to help ensure that they are supported at North Middleton. For example, consistent practices of self-love helped to ensure boundaries around making change, and consistent connections to women of color communities helped define a sisterhood that was truly inclusive. In turn, these sisterhoods helped to sustain and foster self-love in each woman and across their communities. The Black feminist theoretical tradition provides a template to see the connections between naming one's experience, individual and collective resistance, and the creation of knowledge by emphasizing the power of wisdom, sisterhood, and self-love (Collins 2000; Smith and Moore 2019).

How women of color survived and thrived at North Middleton redefines student success to include lived experience and the knowledge we gain from it, self-love, and community change. These themes are also claims to knowledge that help to broaden the meanings of diversity, equity, and inclusion in higher education, as well as related concepts in various academic disciplines. The lessons here help challenge how measures of success are traditionally defined through standardized measures, which primarily reflect the experiences of groups with the most structural and social power.

New measures of success do more than lift the voices of women of color. They also make visible knowledge that has been subjugated and left unconsidered in many aspects of social, political, and economic life. Methodologies help us study social life, and paradigms help us interpret our findings, but epistemologies, as theories of knowledge, help us determine what is true. As Collins explains, these are also shaped by relations of power:

> It [epistemology] investigates the standards used to assess knowledge or *why* we believe what we believe to be true. Far from being the apolitical study of truth, epistemology points to the ways in which power relations shape who is believed and why. For example, various descendants of Sally Hemmings, a Black woman owned by Thomas Jefferson, claimed repeatedly that Jefferson fathered her children. These accounts were ignored in favor of accounts advanced by his White progeny. Hemmings's descendants were routinely disbelieved until their knowledge claims were validated by DNA testing. (2000, 252)

As researchers and participant-researchers in the Black feminist tradition, it is our goal to offer these lessons to reflect the truth more precisely about success strategies, which also reveal the strength, resilience, and humanity of women of color. Therefore, this analysis helps contribute to the scholarship that rejects controlling images as dominant explanations for the experiences of Black women and other women of color.

Intersectional analysis that comes from the scholarly tradition of Black feminist thought and women of color intellectuals is much more than a lens to explain our personal experience. It can also be used to better explain social experiences in general. In this case, intersectionality is a paradigm, and its lens helps us to define more thoroughly the concept of student success. Intersectionality offers insight into experiences typically kept invisible—what women of color know to be true. In this context, how our participants offer lessons/strategies in achievement should be seen as contributions and advancements in knowledge. As agents of knowledge, our study participants helped to change and advance diversity, equity, and inclusion at North Middleton. They should be credited for these efforts, and institutions of higher education, especially those that are predominantly white, should all take note. As Jackie said, "Wake up, class has already begun."

CHAPTER 6

Diversity Solutions

Redefining Student Success

Recall Stephanie, a Black woman discussed in the very first chapter. Stephanie appeared to be a model student: she had a high GPA, attended all her classes, and was very involved in cocurricular activities. At the same time, she was not happy and started to regret her decision to attend North Middleton. Stephanie talked to a professor she considered "good enough," but she really wished she could talk to a professor who was also a woman of color, because she knew that person would fully understand her experiences. Stephanie chose North Middleton because she thought it would be much more diverse than it was, but she instead found herself unable to relate to most of her professors and her peers. She was exhausted and emotionally drained, but she often "pushed through" to manage each day. Pushing through felt frustrating, however, and exacerbated her feelings of isolation. She didn't like that she wasn't standing up for herself and for other women of color.

Given what we now know, let's reconsider Stephanie's experience at North Middleton. How would it have changed if the university had centered the experience of women of color undergraduates? What would it have felt like to not have her success on paper marred by persistent feelings of isolation and doubt? What would it have felt like to have not just momentary relief from venting to a sympathetic professor, but consistent feelings of connection with others? What if, instead of only being seen as success on paper, Stephanie had been seen for her full, authentic being? What would it have looked like if, even at a PWI, she had felt seen and centered for all her lived experiences?

Traditional measures of being a successful college student have been defined from the experiences of people in privileged groups. However, as we have discussed in this book, the experiences of Stephanie and other women of color students reshape what it means to be a thriving undergraduate. Redefining student success would require that higher education professionals deconstruct traditional measures, as well as include a consistent practice that aspires to diversity, equity, and inclusion (Ahmed 2012). Our participants are correct in knowing that being successful shouldn't have to mean mitigating a daily normal of abuse and harm. These women also know that universities are only successful when they ensure a climate that consistently seeks out their perspectives to improve diversity, equity, and inclusion strategies, but does not exploit them in the process.

Lived experience changes what we know, especially when they challenge the dominant explanations that come from socially privileged vantage points considered normal for all people. Black and women of color feminist scholars have long accounted for how people in marginalized positions have double consciousness, triple consciousness, and an insider-outsider view into the function of multiple intersecting systems of oppression. This consciousness allows marginalized individuals to see how their oppressors view them alongside their own view of themselves. Black feminist scholars in particular demonstrate how this perspective develops our knowledge of social systems that see through the epistemological lies of whiteness and other systems of oppression. Moving the voices of women of color undergraduates from margins to center provides more precise explanations of equity issues on campus. Without this knowledge, diversity, equity, and inclusion strategies are partial at best and harmful at worst.

Women of color from various backgrounds have unique standpoints that offer information previously invisible to higher education professionals, most of whom are white. Our research participants understood intersecting systems of oppression because they lived them, and they had not been socialized to be an oppressor in race and gender systems of oppression. As bell hooks explains,

> As a group, Black women are in an unusual position in this society, for not only are we collectively at the bottom of the occupational ladder, but our overall status is lower than that of any other group. Occupying such a position, we bear the brunt of sexist, racist, and classist oppression. At the same time, we are the group that has not been socialized to assume the role of exploiter/oppressor in that we are allowed no institutionalized "other" that we can exploit or oppress. (1984, 16)

This knowledge from lived experiences corrects dominant practices and norms that may appear "natural" to privileged groups but are oppressive to all others. Centering the lived experiences, perspectives, and knowledge of women of color undergraduates would also provide space for universities to trust them. Shifting from margins to center means that predominantly white institutions of higher education would consider women of color undergraduates on their own terms and as reliable epistemic agents (hooks 1984).

Trust Women of Color Students

Our research participants knew what was good for them and what they needed to succeed at North Middleton. To demonstrate the importance of listening to women of color undergraduates, let's consider Khadijah's retelling of meetings with white advisers at North Middleton on two separate occasions. When discussing options for graduate school with one adviser, Khadijah felt dismissed:

> ADVISOR: Well, what do you want to go to grad school for?
>
> KHADIJAH: Oh, I want to go for marketing.
>
> ADVISOR: No.
>
> KHADIJAH: Why not?
>
> ADVISOR: You don't need to go to grad school.
>
> KHADIJAH: But I *want* to go to grad school. So how can you *assist* me so I can go to grad school?
>
> ADVISOR: But you don't need to go to grad school. Why are you going to grad school with an art major?

At this point in the conversation, the adviser clearly didn't think Khadijah's decision to go to graduate school for marketing was correct. Khadijah indicated that a professor had told her the same thing, but she still wanted to pursue graduate school for marketing because she didn't want to go for art and be pushed into teaching. A graduate degree in marketing would also offer her more job opportunities and look great on her résumé.

During her interview with us, Khadijah mentioned that she would have completed the coursework for a marketing minor to complement her graphic design major, but North Middleton didn't have that minor. Thus she decided to pursue a graduate marketing degree to gain those skills and credentials.

> She explained to her advisor: My professor said that too because I'm going to have a bunch of competition with business majors and finance majors, people who already have marketing classes. So, I'm like, but if I'm up for that competition, you can't tell me what I want to do. So why are you steering me away from getting that extra degree?
>
> To which the advisor responded: Well, you're an art major, I understand that. But a lot of the graphic design field has to go with marketing. So it will be great if you take classes. In frustration, Khadijah stated to us: Instead of me taking undergraduate classes, why don't I just get a graduate degree? And that'd be way better! And they just kind of denied it. But to me it made sense.

The advisers likely saw their recommendations as well meaning, but what would the exchange have looked like if they had actually listened to Khadijah? Khadijah's professor and her adviser tried to counsel her about graduate school, but due to their failure to center her in these sessions, she felt unheard and dismissed. During her interview with us, Khadijah analyzed why she thought she had been steered her away from a graduate degree in marketing: "I think, well, I personally thought it was just coming from a spot where it's like, you know, well, why spend that extra money?" However, North Middleton didn't have a marketing minor. Khadijah knew that going to graduate school would allow her to fill that knowledge gap. The professor and adviser thought they were being helpful in this instance, but they were in fact being hurtful. They dismissed her viewpoint, thinking that they knew what was best for Khadijah and wanted to protect her. By stating that she shouldn't pursue further education because of competition, the professor and adviser doubted her abilities.

Khadijah was a highly motivated individual and was involved in many activities on campus. She had come to her decision in a thoughtful manner. She knew that having a degree in both graphic design and marketing would make her a marketable person. She knew what she wanted careerwise and also had a close family friend who had graduated with a marketing major. The advisers lacked vision and held beliefs that got in the way of supporting Khadijah in the way she needed to be supported. They could not see what she saw in herself—a capable person who could get into a graduate marketing degree program. What would it have looked like if North Middleton's professors and advisers had heard and respected our participants for their ambitions and goals? What would it have meant for our participants to not have to consistently defend themselves, but instead be treated as full agents who knew themselves and who must be listened to if we want to ensure diversity, equity, and inclusion?

Give Credit Where Credit Is Due

In every campus tour of North Middleton, there is a stop at one of the university's most celebrated statues as evidence of its commitment to diversity. Prospective white students may find this statue interesting if they notice it all. In contrast, prospective students of color may notice the statue *and* take note of its meaning to society and to their personal histories. It would indicate to them that diversity, equity, and inclusion are highly valued at North Middleton. It would help affirm that they are about to enroll in a college that deeply values them and their experience as *central* to the campus, and that will make them feel welcome and at home. Yet, after spending only a short time on campus, our participants considered this statue part of a false promise to them, which they experienced as a larger web of deceit.

Given what we now know, let's consider this story from a different view. How would the narrative change if you knew that this statue came from the vision of one Black woman faculty member who hoped it would evoke awe and inspiration for everyone at North Middleton? What would you think if you knew that one small but mighty group of African American faculty and staff made this vision a reality? Can you imagine how North Middleton's promise of equity and inclusion would have been strengthened if this specific history had accompanied the university's celebration of the statue?

Larise explained how it felt different to know that people like her built this statue, but also to know that North Middleton did not give credit where credit was due: "Like when this girl was talking about the statue on campus and one of her teachers told her that it was not funded by North Middleton. It was actually a bunch of African American people who came together to do it because North Middleton didn't want to build it. North Middleton doesn't express the fact that Black people built that statue and raised their hard-earned money, doctors, lawyers. It should be educated to people that my culture built this thing." Larise makes clear how important it was for her and everyone at North Middleton to know this history. Sharing this story with the entire university community would demonstrate value for the contributions of people of color and reduce harm. Without this history, the statue is simply an act of appropriation by North Middleton and further evidence that it is a white, masculine, elite space instead of a space that is "home to all."

Larise's viewpoints demonstrate how North Middleton failed to support the efforts of people of color as central to its operations. It was not North Middleton that created this statue, but a small group of African American people just like Larise herself. As historian Dr. tonya thames-taylor makes clear, efforts like these are examples of radical resistance, and to make them visible is powerful. She further states, "To insert ourselves and our politics into a narrative is revolution manifested."

What impact would it have for the entire university community to know the who and how of diversity, equity, and inclusion efforts? What would it mean specifically for students of color to know how often it was "their people who built this thing"? Many predominantly white institutions have a long commitment to diversity, equity, and inclusion. These commitments are sometimes symbolic and sometimes structurally based. They can be traced over time and emphasized during specific periods of social turmoil and unrest. In this book, we have outlined the differences between promises of diversity, accomplishments of diversity, and aspirations for diversity (Ahmed 2012). Under the worst conditions, diversity is part of a neoliberal marketing strategy to gain capital. Under the best conditions, how-

ever, blind spots about diversity are unintentional and invisible via assumed whiteness and other identities of privilege. Institutions that fail women of color students are often simultaneously characterized by exploitative neoliberal practices
and well-meaning intentions to accomplish equity. In this project, we have tried to
learn from the inevitable failures of even the most well meaning of institutions.

What We've Learned

By listening to and centering the voices of women of color undergraduates, we
learned that North Middleton's approach to measuring and celebrating diversity, equity, and inclusion rendered their pain invisible. How North Middleton
proudly recruited and successfully graduated women of color students did not reduce racism, sexism, homophobia, and xenophobia. Moreover, the burden of cultural awareness programming was in large part conducted by multicultural student
organizations. Students initiated this programming because they themselves felt its
necessity, but they did not have training or resources. It was women of color students who did this bridging work on racism, which was an undue burden but also
left the intersections of race and gender invisible. The only way to see these costs
is to listen to those closest to them. Without the voices of women of color undergraduates, North Middleton and other similar institutions would not have seen
or have been able to consider how identity informs political, economic, and social
life, including any bias we may inherit from privileged identities (Combahee River
Collective 1983).

We were reminded that the "personal as political" as identity based and as a
praxis for resistance is a method that would help North Middleton and could help
any institution that aspires to be diverse, equitable, and inclusive. First grounded in
the experiences and knowledge of women of color, personal-as-political methodology helped create later methods of equity and inclusion: identity politics, intersectionality, and the relationship between voice, resistance, and knowledge. Black
feminist epistemology in particular makes it clear how self-love comes from dialogue with other women of color. The epistemology also clarifies how self-love and
dialogue foster an ethics of caring that supports all types of social and economic
justice, because the personal as political makes visible knowledge that has been reduced or left out of traditional explanations of social, political, and economic life.
In other words, the personal as political extends existing epistemologies and helps
us all see more truth.

We discovered that it is imperative that predominantly white institutions of
higher education not take success for granted. Instead, when we investigate success, we see both the ugly underbelly of bridge work and the daily normal, as well

as the success strategies of self-love and collective community-based empowerment. Our participants exemplified their legacy of the strength and resilience of
women of color. Like those before them, they knew that self-love would free them
from internalizing controlling images, exploitation, and harm, creating space for
actions that helped them survive, succeed, and thrive. Self-love, as a political act, as
informed by lived experience, as an act of thriving, must be included in definitions
of student success and considered important contributions to social justice theory
and praxis.

We have shown that institutions must develop new definitions and measures
of success. There is a great need for more allocation of resources, since women of
color students do not always feel supported at predominantly white institutions.
There also need to be initiatives to help improve the campus climate, because
women of color oftentimes feel microaggressions and discomfort from their peers.
In order to ensure that these students thrive on campus and use their full potential,
some changes must take place. In order to be successful, predominantly white institutions of higher education must devise strategies that are further reaching than
what was occurring at the time of our study. Saying that students are welcomed
on campus and that the university celebrates diversity is not enough. There must
be tangible material, emotional, and social support that consistently addresses the
multiple issues that women of color students face on college campuses.

What follows are specific recommendations offered by our research participants, but we would be remiss if we did not first state our limitations. Due to
the nature of ethnographic research, which depends in large part on purposeful
sampling, we were unable to speak to, with, or on behalf of women of color who
come from a wide variety of lived experiences. Although much is certainly missing,
most notable to us is the lack of information from Indigenous and undocumented
women, as well as findings about women who had self-identified as international.
That said, this lack of data on the lived experiences of Indigenous, undocumented,
and international women of color students is in itself an important finding, especially when we discovered that North Middleton sat on Native land and had consistently highlighted its global reach in its promotional materials. In other words,
limitations are also telling. They are continued evidence of the condition of invisibility and the act of silencing, and, like success, they must be consistently considered, investigated, and explained.

Given these shortcomings, it is only appropriate that we follow Sara Ahmed's
call to use language of "aspiration" rather than "accomplishment" not just in diversity, equity, and inclusion strategies in higher education, but also in our own work
(2012). What we mean is that we deeply encourage a close read of this entire project: its recommendations, but also its limits, and we ask that readers consistently
ask themselves, "What is missing here?" Although we are deeply indebted to all

those who moved this project along, we hope to avoid seeing it as one that accomplishes anything, but rather as one that is a contribution to a path that is deeply rooted and forward moving.

Recommendations

The following suggestions were gleaned from and categorized based on the data. To model what it means to center women of color students, we took their words, thoughts, and suggestions seriously. They knew what institutional support and change looked like for them, and we honor that in this book. The recommendations listed are the most salient themes from the observations of our participants.

Center Women of Color Students

A lot of women of color students felt devalued and hypervisible/invisible at North Middleton. That might not have been North Middleton's intention, but that was the lived reality of participants in our study, as we have explained throughout this book. Just as individuals have blind spots, so do institutions. It is not enough to say "you are welcome here." It is not enough to have more diverse people walking on campus. Efforts must be made to see these students, really see them, in their totality. The most well-meaning people and institutions can miss the mark, be oblivious to how their actions impact others, and not see the effects of their one-size-fits-all approach.

Institutions must be more conscious of how women of color students are simultaneously hypervisible and invisible in white, masculine, elite institutions. Centering women of color students would mean that universities consistently acknowledge the legacy of work that women of color have done to better their campuses, and also ensure that they support their students in ways that the students have identified. This provides a bottom-up approach where institutional support and change are informed and guided by those who have typically been put at the margins. In bringing the margin to center, programs and initiatives are richer, more inclusive, and beneficial for all. Students recommended three ways North Middleton could center their experience: (1) support multicultural Greek life, (2) support multicultural organizations and remove the burden of bridge work, and (3) make sure the classroom is a safer space for women of color students.

Support Multicultural Greek Organizations

The role of the Office of Fraternity and Sorority Life (also known as the Office of Greek Life) is to support all Greek organizations, whether they are part of the Multicultural Greek Organizations (MGO), the Interfraternity Council (IFC), or the Panhellenic Council (PHC). However, women of color students were often asked to bridge the gap between the MGO and the mainstream, predominantly white fraternities/sororities (IFC and PHC). Allie in chapter 3 described the double standards that were placed on her sorority, explaining, "We're not forced but it's kind of put upon us that we need to participate in the interfraternity council's thing." Women of color students often thought that the office did not support them in the ways that they needed.

Participants identified that North Middleton could support women of color students by providing financial and institutional assistance to students of color in Greek life. Participants explained that the Multicultural Greek Organizations (MGO) were much smaller in member size and financial resources than the predominantly white councils, such as the IFC and the Panhellenic Council (PHC). Some PHC sororities had about seventy members, while MGO sororities had about ten members. Multicultural sororities were also not seen as part of the wider Greek life umbrella even though they technically were. Our participants felt that there was Greek life and then there were the organizations they were part of.

In chapter 3, Allie highlighted the different treatment and the double standards placed on her sorority when its members sought to interact with other Greek organizations: "Part of the issue of why they're treated differently unlike the white orgs is that they don't have the means to participate in a larger group. The university should offer community building initiatives to bridge the gap between the IPC/Panhellenic orgs and the MGO. Whoever organizes Greek Week should lead that effort." The Office of Greek Life should have been mindful about not expecting or pressuring women of color members of multicultural Greek organizations to be a bridge to the predominantly white Greek organizations. Going forward, departments like this could frame their efforts through an equity lens and find ways to place the responsibility for unity on the institution.

That said, expectations for unity should never be forced on students of color in predominantly white institutions of higher education because students in multicultural Greek organizations need their safe spaces too. The biggest issue we heard from women of color students was the fact that the Office of Greek Life kept asking them to do things without ever asking how it could help them in return. The office had also made assumptions about the membership in all the organizations that weren't entirely true. For example, there were students of color in predominantly white organizations and white students in the historically multicultural organizations. Women of color students explained how the Office of Greek Life took it for granted that unity between historically multicultural organizations and predominantly white ones would accomplish its diversity goals. But in doing so, the office ignored the participation of women of color students in the predominantly white organizations.

If the office is to serve *all* students in Greek life and all Greek life organizations, then it must change its approach to ensure that it is actually serving women of color students in the ways that those students identify. Instead of staff asking these women to do bridge work for unity, they should ask instead, "How can we help and support you?" The office should hear and learn from women of color students because they know what's best for themselves and the organizations they participate in.

In addition to centering the voices of women of color members, departments like these could hire alumnae of or current women of color students in Greek life as consultants to develop community-building initiatives. This would also help support another recommendation given to us by our participants that we'll discuss later in this chapter—increasing staff of color across all departments on campus. Because the Office of Greek Life staff at North Middleton is mostly white, they might not have even thought about the different factors to consider in building unity. They are less likely to anticipate the unintended consequences of their approach because of their own blind spots exacerbated by white permanence at North Middleton. If there were staff of color, especially staff of color who were alumni of Multicultural Greek Organizations, there would be voices at the table that could speak to better approaches for unity.

Support Multicultural Organizations and Remove the Burden of Bridge Work

Just as they had recommended to the Office of Greek Life, our participants expressed wanting more and broader institutional support for multicultural student organizations. Many women of color students in our study did bridge work through educational programming and unofficial cultural awareness events hosted by their organizations. We call these efforts "bridge work" because they involved free labor that ultimately served North Middleton's goals for diversity, equity, and inclusion. On one hand, many of our participants felt called to do this work, but on the other hand, they felt like they had no choice, given the climate of North Middleton's campus. This last point was a problem. In chapter 3, Ari articulated it, stating that as a student leader, she considered herself a teacher and had to be open to being uncomfortable. She further expressed that she had to be open to looking at issues whichever way her peers were, and that she had to "attack everything with kindness."

Student affairs could take some of the burden off student organizations that do educational programming. That way, these students could have programming allowing them to connect with one another. Financial resources could be provided to help individuals from these groups create such plans for themselves. Student affairs could start an initiative or division for campus-wide educational programming regarding diversity, equity, and inclusion issues. To minimize the labor of women of color students, the university could also outsource informative programming from people outside the campus. Another solution would be to pay students to do this work. Taking the burden of educating the wider campus community off of women of color would allow these students to focus and have programming to connect with one another and foster community care.

Make the Classroom a Safer Space
for Women of Color Students

Predominantly white universities need to make sure that the classroom is a safer space for women of color undergraduates, ensuring that they aren't rendered invisible, and that they aren't made hypervisible as course material. Women of color students need to feel like they belong in the college classroom just as much as white students do. This could be achieved by centering the perspectives of women of color through texts rather than tokenizing students in class discussion. As described in chapter 3, our women of color participants were made the go-to people, a role that left them feeling hypervisible but also ignored and dismissed. White students were not expected to be the spokespeople for their race / ethnic background. However, when racial events happened, women of color students had to talk about them and make it easier for white people to talk about them. Women of color undergraduates felt an expectation to take on the role of the resident expert, which made them feel tokenized and which also trivialized their experiences.

In the classroom, white professors, even the well-intentioned ones, can have blind spots. Intentionally or unintentionally, the white professors at North Middleton might have had expectations for how women of color students should show up that were not the same expectations they had for other students. In their quest to keep the classroom student centered, professors might have had the opposite effect: othering women of color students or making them hypervisible.

Our participants overwhelmingly agreed that there should have been more literature and film representation of people of color in all their classes. They indicated that the perspectives of women of color should not have been placed in the margins in the curriculum, the course content, texts, videos, and films. Women of color students should have their voices centered through course materials instead of having to become "the text" in the classroom. This way, students of color would more consistently hear their stories, and white students would be exposed to different perceptions and perspectives. By centering women of color students through text, the responsibility for education does not fall on those students. White students can learn about the lived experience of people of color through course materials.

While centering women of color students includes diversifying the curriculum, it also involves enhancing teaching methods in the to combat bias, racism, sexism, and other systems of oppression that our participants often experienced in class discussion. The permanence of elite masculine whiteness at predominantly white institutions of higher education fosters a very limited worldview in the classroom. That is why it is imperative that white professors call out bias, sexism, racism, and other hate speech, even if it's unintentional, as it occurs and as part of a "call in" learning process (Ross 2019). To make the classroom a safer space, faculty should not expect students of color to identify instances of identity-based harms. Instead, educators should anticipate that these harms could occur and be prepared to handle them appropriately when they do. Through training, professors can develop the tools to help mitigate instances of racism, sexism, and other identity-based harm while keeping the classroom student centered. Professors can change their pedagogy and approaches to teaching so that both calling out bias and calling in students to challenge it are integrated into the curriculum. Doing so will help facilitate a safer space for women of color students.

Foster a Community of Women of Color, for Women of Color, and by Women of Color

The women of color students we interviewed yearned for community with others. Navigating white, masculine, elite spaces, bridging labor, and the daily normal diminished the time, energy, and resources these women could have devoted to developing safe zones and community events dedicated to self and community care. In our study, students identified three ways to foster that community for themselves: (1) support/redefine mentorship programs, (2) establish safe zones/spaces, and (3) dedicate spaces to educating and supporting one another instead of the university.

Support/Redefine Mentorship Programs

The existing mentorship program at North Middleton (and similar programs at other predominantly white institutions of higher education) should be redefined based on our findings and analysis. Peer mentors should be matched by race / ethnicity / cultural background and gender, and these pair groups should be kept small—two or three people in each. Significant literature shows mentorship matching by identity is not as salient as it seems (Buffy Smith 2015). However, scholarship also shows that having a mentor of the same race adds ease and a sense of trust, and that having a common cultural foundation between mentor and mentee can be helpful for "clear communication, baseline understanding of circumstances, and the feeling that someone has 'been there'" (Campbell and Campbell 2007, 389).

Women of color undergraduates in our study asserted that they sought mentors who were women of color, who shared both their race *and* their gender. However, because North Middleton did not prioritize these types of matches, some participants believed that their mentor matches in the program failed. For example, a theme we heard from international women of color students was how they benefited from knowing someone on campus who had experienced the same culture shock they did upon coming to a white and American space like North Middleton. Tessa, an African woman, said that what helped her most in transitioning to a new school in a new country was having an African friend who came from the same university back home in Europe. She knew someone who was going through the same experience that she was. If she was in the mentorship program and was matched with a Black American woman, the Black American woman mentor could connect due to her insider status when it comes to race, but would still have that outsider status based on ethnicity and immigration status.

This is not to say that having the same race/ethnicity and gender automatically means an effective mentor-mentee relationship will happen. However, it can help with trust and communication due to shared cultural background and understanding. The mentorship experience is richer when mentors can also relate to navigating experiences at the intersection of their race, ethnicity, cultural background, and gender.

North Middleton and other predominantly white institutions of higher education should improve current mentorship programs for students of color to ensure that mentees' needs are met and their development is encouraged in a variety of ways (academically, socially, professionally, etc.). Women of color students need support in navigating predominantly white institutions, especially if they are the first in their families to attend one. In a predominantly white institution of higher education like North Middleton, students navigate academia and the social scene with their peers, deal with the daily normal, and learn how to develop their skill sets so that they can start their careers once they graduate. Mentorship programs can help women of color with each of these different areas and help them navigate other resources. To have that kind of well-rounded approach requires a mentor to devote quality time to a mentee.

Based on the data, we argue that there should be a lower mentor-mentee ratio in mentorship programs to ensure that mentors are able to devote quality time to each mentee. At the time of our research study, there was a high mentor-mentee ratio at North Middleton, approximately five to one. Students complained that they didn't get to spend much time with their mentors. One participant told of meetings occurring only four times a year; another shared that most of the communication with her mentor was via text message. A high mentor-mentee ratio spread mentors thin and prevented mentees from developing quality connections with them. A high ratio also prevented mentees from feeling supported. To achieve a lower ratio, universities would need to provide more funding to the department that runs the mentorship program so that current peer mentors aren't spread thin.

At the time of this study, the program at North Middleton had only included first-year students in its mentee criteria. To really support women of color students, the criteria should be expanded so that mentorship can be accessible for all students, ensuring that transfer students and international students could actively participate in programs as well. Those two populations may need even more assistance when coming to a university with a limited social network and support.

In addition, predominantly white institutions of higher education should create and sustain university-wide cascade-style mentoring programs for and by self-identified women of color. They should be led by women of color. With a cascading mentorship model, women of color undergraduates receive mentoring from more senior students or faculty/staff while at the same time providing it to younger students, like those in high school.

Our study was inspired by a similar program at North Middleton. There, fourteen college students were assigned a faculty/staff mentor and matched with high school mentees who had submitted applications to participate. The program kicked off with a welcome lunch. Then each trio stayed in touch with one another through the course of one year and recorded at least one conversation about their experiences with education and empowerment. The group of college students also met every two weeks to build community and share tips on mentorship. The program culminated with an event at the end of the academic year that included inspiring quotes from all the mentees. It was a highly successful endeavor, and students truly believed that they benefited from it. Everyone wanted it to continue, but more institutional support and resources were needed for that to happen. The cascading mentorship program is an example of a successful model that predominantly white institutions of higher education could implement to provide tangible support to women of color students on campus.

Establish Safe Zones/Spaces

Participants recommended establishing safe zones/spaces as another way to foster community for and by women of color. Ari described this plan:

> I think we need a safe zone. That's it. My job and when I was on campus and I was going through my things, I didn't have anyone to turn to, at least I didn't feel like it. And people were like oh, there's resources. You can go to the women's center. I didn't feel welcome at the women's center. Nothing they did, it's just, I guess I'm just so taught to be isolated, to do it by myself, to do it on my own, that it was weird to ask for help. At that time, even when I think about it now, I wouldn't go to the women's center, I feel like that's just not for me. I guess it's more in my mind. It's like I'm taught to automatically assume I'm not accepted until I feel like I am. So, women's center never did anything for me to feel like I could go there, especially when I was there. And when I was starting to feel comfortable, it was because of the students and the atmosphere they created. But when the director came, she changed the atmosphere, she said that you couldn't have your friends here.

As we heard from Ari, the Women's Center office could have done more to ensure that women of color students felt welcomed. Ari only felt accepted and comfortable going to the center when she connected with students who hung out there. The students, not the staff, were the ones who created an inviting atmosphere.

Ari and her peers—other students who went to the center—had the idea of creating an organization called Three Strikes. Three Strikes means that you are LGBTQ+, a woman, and a woman of color. The students and Ari saw a need for space for LGBTQ+ women of color to connect and have community. Rather than supporting the idea, the center director discouraged them from hanging out in the Women's Center. Her reasoning was to ensure that the facility was a safe space for students who had experienced sexual assault or rape and needed to meet privately with staff.

Although the Women's Center's staff members meant well in their quest to create a safe space for survivors, as Ari pointed out, their intentions had the opposite effect:

> She wanted it to be safe zone, which I understood, but from a student perspective it didn't make sense. She wanted it to be zone for instance if a student got raped, they could come in there and say I got raped and then people could say yeah, let me talk to you. But I was like, what, no, nobody is going to do that. First of all, for them to even tell anybody are they going to want to tell a complete stranger or are

they wanting to go to the center, I think they would want to be around a group of women students, but she didn't want it to be just a place to hang out.

The director's decision thwarted the momentum that could have gotten the Three Strikes idea off the ground. Ari identified a gap in student services that would have helped LGBTQ+ women of color: spaces that acknowledge and see the intersection of women of color who identify as queer/nonbinary/trans. Those who want to support women of color students must be mindful of how they talk about them because they are not a monolith. It's important to have safe spaces/zones for all types of women of color. Staff and the wider university must be intentional in how they create these spaces, as they should accurately support women of color students' needs.

It's very important for students of color to be in spaces that are only for them (Bessette 2014). Participants shared that in instances where white people were welcomed in people-of-color spaces, they eventually claimed the areas as their own, dominated them, or took over. Larise analyzed an instance where a white woman student who attended Black Student Union events wished more white students attended: "I feel like that could go either way because if you just have white people go to the Black student union, that just destroys the whole message and what it is supposed to be about. This school is a predominantly white school and just to have African Americans to have an outlet."

Women of color students deserve to have spaces that are made for them and by them. Safe zones/spaces can look like specific programs catered to self-identified women of color so that they can have an area for community, support, and mentorship. North Middleton did not need to start from scratch. Programs already in place could have been developed and better resourced to provide additional support and security for our participants. Larise explained the importance of the Black Student Union:

> It's good to have that one place where we can all come together and listen, we're all Black and we can all talk about different things: hip hop, music, race, sexism. Being in a school that's predominantly white, it's a good thing to have. It's good for Black people to have their foundation, there are already so many programs where everyone can come. I think it's just that I came from a whole Black environment and now I am in a PWI and I can come back to this only Black space, I think it's just good to be around people who are going through the same thing I am. It wouldn't be the same.

Larise observed that an "only Black space," one that is solely for Black people, is "a good thing to have." Any area dedicated to fostering community among women of color should emphasize educating and supporting these students, not educating the whole university. To avoid involving these students in unpaid labor promoting diversity, equity, and inclusion for the university, institutions should ensure that these spaces remain ones that provide support for women of color. These spaces need to center communities by and for women of color; any other external educational effort must be secondary unless it is better institutionally resourced.

As one example of helping women of color build their own spaces, our participants suggested having events where women of color staff and faculty can meet with other women of color on campus. Women of color students wanted to see more of and connect with professors who looked like them. Academia is a tough place for women of color professors. Professors are already overburdened and overworked, and they may feel alone or isolated. By holding these events, universities can foster community between students and faculty and energize them both. Women of color students can see that they do have a place at North Middleton and that there is a way forward if they choose a career path in academia.

Odette shared how her experience connecting with a Black woman faculty member on campus during her time at North Middleton helped her succeed:

> Taking Dr. Abara's *Philosophy of Race* course was such an incredible experience. I was lucky enough to take two of her courses while at North Middleton. From long conversations about Frantz Fanon and the Black experience to navigating post undergraduate life as a woman of color, she became a mentor to me. I often came to her when I had problems on campus and she not only listened but was there to provide me with support, sound advice and large amounts of Thai food when needed. This is a relationship that we have been able to maintain since I graduated, from being able to attend an array of conferences for Black women in philosophy to helping her organize a book club for African writers.

Having a Seat at the Table in a More Formal and Regular Way

Often reserved for individuals with the power to make decisions, having a proverbial seat at the table has become a representation of influence, credibility, and status afforded to some individuals. In other words, when individuals are allowed a seat at the table, they have the chance to be heard and to create change within various systems. Moreover, being welcomed at this table means that the views and perspectives of all at the table are valued and considered by the systems that have established it.

Our participants were expected to partake in leadership roles that pushed

North Middleton's goals of diversity, but they were often left out of conversations pertaining to their treatment at the university. Women of color students did not have any input when it came to shaping university-wide diversity, equity, and inclusion efforts. In fact, gaining a seat at the table was often difficult.

Veronica explained how North Middleton excluded women of color and other marginalized groups from positions of power when it pertained to the formulation of diversity, equity, and inclusion programming:

> I want to know why it's a secretive thing and you're not including us. This affects us, this is about us, it's going to affect other students like us, it's impacting us way more than people who are involved and who are doing the research. And going through the report and seeing the suggestions, there are so many things you don't know. Like housing for example, a lot of your students aren't coming back because they have nowhere to live, like where are they going to live. I am not going to pay $10,000 to live in a residence hall, but that's all where you can put me and then I cannot commute from Philly because I don't have a car. There are so many things.

Veronica's statement highlights a claim supported by many of our participants: the perspectives and knowledge of women of color were not held in the same regard as those of their white counterparts. The university's programs, strategies, and solutions pertaining to race, class, and gender were formulated without the insights and opinions of this group.

Based on our participants' feedback, we propose that North Middleton University and all predominantly white institutions of higher education guarantee women of color students a formal voice in the planning of diversity, equity, and inclusion initiatives. This means taking their issues and experiences on campus more seriously and involving them in all planning stages. Repositioning women of color in this role should not be done symbolically, which would trivialize their experiences. Our research shows that ignoring the lived experiences of women of color undergraduates created further instances where our participants felt invisible.

To ensure that women of color students are represented in any diversity, equity, and inclusion efforts established by the institution, North Middleton University could create positions on university-wide diversity committees to include students from marginalized groups. Like those holding other committee positions, these representatives would be voted in by their peers and serve as the voice for all students of color. Representatives would have the ability to present proposed initiatives crafted by students of color to the larger committee. By creating or reconstructing the diversity committee, the university could build genuine connections and receive guidance from individuals who are often left out of conversations about issues that most directly affect them. Furthermore, the development and cultivation of this leadership position would reduce the instances where women of color students feel tokenized simply for the sake of diversifying the campus.

Another way to ensure that women of color have a space at the table is to provide formal areas for women of color students to talk to faculty, staff, and administrators. This should be done in ways that recognize the knowledge and contributions these women possess when it comes to establishing diversity, equity, and inclusion programming. The establishment of these formal spaces would not only allow for honest dialogue to occur, but it would also create a shift in community accountability by centering women of color and other marginalized groups. More importantly, the creation of these spaces would also allow women of color to be seen by the university, which would aid in establishing a more dynamic relationship with communities of color.

Jillian explained how transformative it can be for women of color to have direct channels to administrative spaces and have their voices heard within the university: "I actually spoke in front of the board about diversity so that was nice because it showed me that although they might not openly say it, there were faculty and staff that do care. The president was there, different department chairs were there. Program directors and the recruitment head. So it was nice that they were asking us questions about how to get more diversity. It was nice because they wanted to know how to let the students of color know that they do care, so that was a big improvement that I saw because I was there."

University-Level Diversity-Aspirational Policies

Given the role that access to higher education plays in improving opportunities for people of color and other marginalized groups, there is a growing need for universities to improve the educational experience for all students of color. We know that some institutions are well meaning and do want to support students of color. That's why North Middleton and other predominantly white schools must approach diversity, equity, and inclusion work from a diversity-aspirational mindset (Ahmed 2012). To promote social inclusion and cultural diversity, regulatory frameworks and public policy should be created. This work is iterative. It isn't about perfection or reaching a goal and being done with it. One can think of it as an institutional growth mindset. To achieve this goal of diversity aspiration, we have outlined four components that should be considered when institutions are formulating diversity, equity, and inclusion policies.

First, new procedures should be more specific, encompassing implementation that can be seen at every level and department of the university. Our participants have stated that many of the current diversity, equity, and inclusion efforts created by North Middleton were too broad. The creation of policies in each department would formally address the varying experiences of many of these students, especially those who majored in the sciences and prelaw. Unlike programs in women's and gender studies, African American studies, and social work, science and law programs tended to avoid discussions about systematic racism, other oppressions, and the various ways these can affect students in the department. An intersectional approach should be explored while formulating classes and in analyzing the department culture.

Second, our participants have stated their belief that North Middleton created many diversity, equity, and inclusion goals to meet its diversity objectives but failed to assess how students were impacted by these efforts. Working in conjunction with previous recommendations, diversity, equity, and inclusion language and programs should not be used to celebrate the institution's claims about diversity (Ahmed 2012). Instead, the university should listen to former and incoming students to learn from the failures of a diversity-accomplished approach. By determining the best way to measure diversity efforts, North Middleton would have the chance to create performance goals that not only address the needs of students of color, but also effectively communicate the university's desire to create a diverse campus. As we have discussed throughout this book, our participants stated that they felt fooled by the university once they became students. They recalled seeing diverse representation of peers on the campus website and brochure when deciding to apply, but they failed to see this diversity once enrolled. Providing women of color students with factual examples of diversity would allow them to make informed decisions about whether to attend the university.

Third, revamping the class curriculum is needed to ensure that the lived experiences of students and faculty of color are not exploited for the sake of educating their white counterparts (e.g., as white professors outsourced the knowledge of our participants to educate white students on identity-based issues). Participating in this additional labor helped to create experiences of being both invisible and hypervisible, which contributed to the daily normal for the students we interviewed. To avoid this, we recommend including intersectional scholars in all courses.

Intersectionality can serve as an important tool that allows students and faculty members to understand the intersecting identities of their peers and the discrimination and oppression they may experience. The concept also emphasizes creating a more equitable and inclusive society by allowing individuals to understand and acknowledge the privileges they themselves hold. This is something not always afforded to students using a traditional educational lens. An intersectional approach will prove essential when identifying and addressing the gaps in the current curriculum. It would provide a richer learning experience to all students and move beyond narrow viewpoints most of them are taught in our educational system.

Veronica discussed the importance of being in classes that represent all ethnic groups, noting how significant it would be for students of color to take courses where they could learn about their history. She stated, "We always learn about these white people in these classes. This is the first time I learned about people that look like me. When I took my first Women and Gender studies class, it was so refreshing to learn about people that looked like me. For so long we have had to learn about white history like Black people haven't done stuff too. So, it was nice to see our people and history being taught." Veronica's sentiment was shared by other women of color at North Middleton. They wanted to see more well-rounded and realistic courses being offered to students. It is therefore important to pay attention to the creation, development, and administration of the current curriculum at predominantly white institutions of higher education, as the groups serving in the planning committees may not be communities of color and may not be familiar with intersectional frameworks. Universities should also expand the process of how courses and course content are crafted.

Fourth, to create policies that effectively promote diversity and inclusion, universities should improve annual campus climate surveys so that they are also guided by intersectional frameworks. At the time of this study, North Middleton's survey had failed to tell the full experiences of students on campus. While it analyzed race, it did not give insight into students' multiple or intersecting identities (such as race and gender). By ignoring these identities, the university was not able to gain a full perspective on the discomfort many individuals endured because of their combined race, ethnicity, and gender. Contextual factors such as sexual orientation and immigration status could also be used by the university to best understand the experiences of students of color.

Results and recommendations entered at the end of campus climate surveys should be made available to the entire university body, and institutions should make clear accountability paths by sharing timelines and budgets. Results should be shared with all, and professors who have expertise in diversity, equity, and inclusion should help design and implement the goals. All professors and students who participate in these efforts, but especially those of color and newer to the university, should be compensated for their work.

Required Education

At the time of this study, North Middleton required students of all majors to take one diversity course. Our participants thought this requirement should be expanded to ensure that all white students on campus learn about anti-racism scholars and frameworks. Our participants recommended increasing the number of required diversity courses from one to three:

1. Students should be required to take Introduction to Women's Studies or a similar class in their first year. Participation in this course will allow students to examine the social construction of gender through intersectional and transnational frameworks, and to explore the experience and history of identity, as well as its influence on one's perspective of various groups.

2. In their first year, students should also be required to take a course on race relations or a similar topic. This class will allow students to comprehend the lived experiences of members belonging to various racial groups. These courses will also promote a cultural practice of recognizing diversity and the need for inclusive and equitable frameworks.

3. In addition, students should be required to take an ethics course in conjunction with diverse communities classes. North Middleton is made up of a majority of white students. Many of these individuals do not have an understanding of race and have spent much of their lives in environments that center whiteness and white-centered Western cultures. This results in racial blindness, which prevents them from seeing their own racial privilege. Participating in an ethics class would also be beneficial for students of color, who may not have learned about their lack of privilege or the systemic forces behind oppression that deeply affect their lives.

More Resources and Support for Indigenous Students, International Students of Color, and Undocumented Students

As supported by our lack of findings, additional information, resources, and support are needed for Indigenous students, international students of color, and undocumented students. As compared with American-born students, these individuals have a different perspective on and experience of navigating identity-based systems of oppression. In their home countries, international women of color students identified themselves as members of the majority; this was even more the case in countries with homogeneous populations. In these instances, race was not a defining identity marker. Coming to the United States was the first instance in which race relations became more salient for international students of color, contributing to the way in which race informed their definitions of self. Our international participants experienced isolation and loneliness like other women of color students did. But they also named language barriers, struggles to assimilate to a new environment and culture, traumas from their home countries, and immigration status as additional obstacles affecting how they experienced campus life.

In addition, North Middleton University is home to a sizable population of undocumented students. Like international students, undocumented individuals at the university have a different experience from their American-born counterparts. Given these students' immigration status, the financial aid resources allocated to them are lacking. These individuals also experience higher rates of poverty that contribute to their financial stresses. Furthermore, they carry the fear of their immigration status being leaked, and they face the risk of deportation. This fear became actualized during the Trump administration, when many undocumented students were being detained by ICE and subsequently deported. During this time, various multicultural organizations at North Middleton created programs to support undocumented students and inform others of the harsh treatment they could experience. One of these events explained the importance of sanctuary cities and provided a forum for the wider campus community to learn more about the lived experiences of undocumented students. It also safely provided undocumented students with legal assistance to navigate immigration issues.

Create Initiatives to Recruit, Hire, and Retain
Women of Color Faculty, Staff, and Counselors

Throughout this book, we have spoken at length about the importance of representation and support and how they can uplift women of color students at North Middleton. Many of our participants felt disconnected from their white professors and other staff at the university. Khadijah's experience with her counselor described in the beginning of this chapter is just one of many examples where women of color students had adverse interactions with white staff. Such encounters could also involve well-intentioned white staff at the university, as these individuals may lack the cultural awareness and lived experience to facilitate the needs of their students of color. As a result, we recommend creating initiatives to recruit, hire, and retain more women of color faculty, staff, and counselors.

Dana explained the need for hiring more faculty of color:

> I think faculty need to be more evenly distributed when it comes to race. . . . I really don't see diversity amongst the faculty unless you get diverse faculty in here, I think that's when your students can be more comfortable, outgoing, and vocal with their needs and their wants and their opinions because that's when they will feel more comfortable. But just to be able to see a Black female in that space would give me more confidence, and would make me be able to talk to her more

in a more comfortable level and just to help with my path because if she can do it and get here that means I can do it and get here too.

Like Dana, many of our participants knew the power of having staff and counselors that looked like them, and who would relate to their life experiences and advocate for them. Due to their lack of knowledge and social location, some white counselors may not deeply understand the intersectional issues that women of color face.

Importantly, there is an intersectional focus in treatment and care to understand how culture and systems of oppression affect the physical and mental health of women of color students. Sam addressed the significance of having counselors of color:

> I had a white man counselor my junior year when I was struggling with my mental health. One challenge I had was my decision to "go natural" and getting negative feedback from my family. My counselor was nice and saw that it was a big deal for me. He didn't understand the significance of "going natural" and wanted to understand my reality more so I had to explain relaxers, the natural hair movement, and the politics of Black hair so he could get it. He did try to understand so I'll give him that. I never felt like he was dismissing my experience per se, but it was uncomfortable sometimes having to explain to this older white guy. I would just feel reminded of how our worlds were so different. I just wanted someone who knew my world. It's a different experience when you have a counselor with your cultural background and gender who just gets what you're talking about and can relate. You feel more understood.

Besides providing support for women of color students, hiring more faculty of color would lessen the load for existing staff of color who are overburdened by their current workload. Focusing on how the university hires and retains women of color faculty, staff, and counselors would also address the existing issues surrounding low retention of these individuals.

Trainings

Women of color undergraduates recommended that North Middleton incorporate a series of diversity, equity, and inclusion trainings to increase the university community's knowledge and awareness of the cultural, racial, and gender differences of students of color. Participants suggested that training be created for everyone, but especially for professors, advisers, students, and peer mentors. These instructions should occur twice during the semester, at the start and end of the term, and be facilitated by people with expertise in the specific topics. Then professors and advising staff should be evaluated on whether they adequately integrate this training into their teaching and advising sessions. To do so, end-of-term evaluations could be expanded to address diversity, equity, and inclusion, offering students a chance to provide their honest opinions on how well professors engage with these issues. Students will have a tangible method to quantify how well diversity goals are being received on campus.

Students should be required to participate in diversity and anti-racism training throughout their undergraduate careers. It is important for white students to not only recognize oppressive systems but also have the tools to deconstruct these systems and understand how they impact people of color at the university. Jillian stressed the importance of providing students with diversity, equity, and inclusion instruction: "[There should be] required training for incoming students on diversity, like the ones we do for alcohol, to provide students [a way] to look at a variety of situations and scenarios that they may not have thought about before. Even if they joke about it and blow it off, at least they were exposed to it somehow." To Jillian's point, all training sessions should be held multiple times throughout students' time at North Middleton to give them a chance to enhance their understanding of the issues and concepts being taught. It should be noted that diversity, equity, and inclusion instruction should not be crafted just to address the university's diversity goals. These programs should be consistent and ongoing to ensure that they address the concerns that our participants have identified throughout this study.

In Sum

Who is succeeding and at what cost? We hope this question will be a consistent touchstone as we all aspire to diversity, equity, and inclusion, both in theory and in practice. While it would seem intuitive to celebrate when a predominantly white institution demonstrates its diversity, accomplishes equity, and appears inclusive, doing so without ensuring that all students, but especially successful women of color students, are supported is a lie at best and harmful at worst. Women of color undergraduates should not be exploited for their labor, nor should institutions carelessly overrely on them. These women should be at all formal institutional discussions of diversity, equity, and inclusion, and they should be heard. Our participants offered important clarifications and corrections to diversity, equity, and inclusion, as well as important insight that redefines the concept of student success. Going forward, we hope that measures of student success will include safe campus climates, emotional and physical well-being, and connection and community for all.

What could make a diversity promise a reality? Our study shows the importance in shifting the conversations about diversity, equity, and inclusion to be "aspirational," not "accomplished" (Ahmed 2012). What this means is that institutions balance between integrated spaces and safe spaces for marginalized people and do not assume that all spaces are for all people at any given time. Administrators should consistently make policies and practices just as visible as discourse and regularly check these for inconsistencies. Administrators, faculty, and staff should be as honest and transparent about the failures of their institutions as they are about the successes. Diversity, equity, and inclusion efforts could keep the celebratory spotlights, but they should be substantiated with ongoing discussions of shortcomings, reflection, and earnest provision of structural support and resources. Persistent elite masculine whiteness should be anticipated and consistently interrogated at all levels everywhere—but most definitely in the spaces of higher education. Success should not only be measured by individual outcomes, but also by community gains and collective solidarity focusing on contributions to the common good over contributions to the market.

The combination of intersectionality with institutional ethnography captured the lived experiences of women of color undergraduates at North Middleton from their perspectives. This methodological synthesis honors their voices, but it also yields important thematic findings that would improve diversity, equity, and inclusion and contribute to current and future social justice scholarship, dialogue, and praxis. We hope this work adds to the long and visionary tradition of feminist scholarship by women of color, Black feminist epistemologies, and intersectionality, all of which correct unilateral explanations of social life. We hope that the theoretical synthesis of emotional labor with critiques of higher education will continue to inspire close analyses of neoliberalism, capital, and exploited labor at all levels of a work organization in higher education.

This said, it is critical to note that we were not the first in coming to the conclusions discussed in this book, nor will we be the last. Rather, we aspire to be an important piece of the puzzle. As we have said throughout, revealing the complexities and contributions of the invisible isn't a one-and-done action, but is ongoing. We tried to honor what renowned sociologist Dr. Kathleen Blee teaches us—to understand and fix a problem, we must study the mundane. In this case, studying and redefining the meaning of "successful student" makes our diversity, equity, and inclusion efforts better, but it also supports our students. All this combined makes it clear how the personal as political is not just an explanation of lived experience, is not just a call to action. Instead, it is a methodology that helps to study the relationship between voice, resistance, and knowledge because it emphasizes the epistemological agency and contributions of people not typically seen.

Shifting the perspectives of women of color undergraduates from margin to center and then centering this wisdom would help predominantly white institutions of higher education improve their diversity, equity, and inclusion efforts. Being in a marginalized group means being able to understand power relations from your own perspective and from the perspective of privileged groups (Collins 2000). As bell hooks reminds us, it is important to recognize the agency that comes from knowing multiple experiences at once:

> Spaces of agency exist for Black people, wherein we can both interrogate the gaze of the Other but also look back, and at one another, naming what we see. The "gaze" has been and is a site of resistance for colonized Black people globally. Subordinates in relations of power learn experientially that there is a critical gaze, one that "looks" to document, one that is oppositional. In resistance struggle, the power of the dominated to assert agency by claiming and cultivating "awareness" politicizes "looking" relations—one learns to look a certain way in order to resist. (1992, 116).

There is power and knowledge in this resistance that universities should aspire to understand in order to value their women of color undergraduates, but also to ensure that their strategies are as effective as they claim.

We hope this book provides some steps in the long journey toward social justice and contributes to knowledge in a wide array of fields. If you are a reader who works at a predominantly white institution of higher education, especially if you are white, we hope you understand the importance of investigating success and not taking it for granted. We hope this book prepares you to create and administer programming that will serve all students of color, even those who appear to not need it. If you are or have ever been a woman of color undergraduate student, this book is for you. We see your successes. We see the burdens imposed on you. We see your strength, endurance, and resilience. But most of all, we see you. We thank you for your time. We thank you for your insights. And we thank you for all your energies every single day.

Demographics

At the time of our study, all our participants identified as cisgender women. What follows is a table that categorizes the race, ethnicity, and sexuality of our interview participants. We collapse some categories to ensure the students' confidentiality. This situation isn't ideal, especially given the themes related to different experiences for women of color international students. A major foundation to our claims is that identity-based experiences inform knowledge—that is, what we know to be "true." This is why we add demographics to quotations throughout the book. One last note: as is the case with all qualitative data, these numbers should not be used to make broad, sweeping generalizations. Rather, they should simply provide context for the themes discussed in this work. We hope the themes and theoretical contributions of this manuscript will inspire writing, research, policy, activism, and everyday conversations.

Race and/or Ethnicity	no.	Sexuality	no.
African American or Black	25	Straight	15
Biracial/multi-racial	9	Lesbian	4
Asian, Asian American, or SE Asian	3	Bisexual	4
International or Latina	8	Not said	22
TOTAL	45		45

BIBLIOGRAPHY

Aguilar, Delia D. 2010. "From Triple Jeopardy to Intersectionality: The Feminist Perplex." *Comparative Studies of South Asia, Africa and the Middle East* 32, no. 2: 415–28.

Ahmed, Sara. 2012. *On Being Included: Racism and Diversity in Institutional Life*. Durham, N.C.: Duke University Press.

Alexander, Jaqui M. 2005. *Pedagogies of Crossing: Meditations on Feminism, Sexual Politics, Memory, and the Sacred*. Durham, N.C.: Duke University Press.

Alexander, Michelle. 2010. *The New Jim Crow: Mass Incarceration in the Age of Colorblindness*. New York: New Press.

Anderson, Elijah. 2015. "The White Space." *Sociology of Race and Ethnicity* 1, no. 1: 10–21. https://doi.org/10.1177/2332649214561306.

———. 2022. *Black in White Space: The Enduring Impact of Color in Everyday Life*. Chicago: University of Chicago Press.

Anderson, Tamara D., and Maya Anderson. 2021. "The Erasure of Black Women." *Journal of Critical Education Policy Studies at Swarthmore College* 8–25.

Anthias, Floya. 2013. "Intersectional What? Social Divisions, Intersectionality and Levels of Analysis." *Ethnicities* 13, no. 1: 3–19.

Antonio, Anthony Lisinc. 2003. "Diverse Student Bodies, Diverse Faculties." *Academe* 89, no. 6: 14–17.

Anzaldúa, Gloria. 1987. *Borderlands / La Frontera: The New Mestiza*. San Francisco, Calif.: Aunt Lute Books.

Beck, Koa. 2021. *White Feminism: From the Suffragettes to the Influencers and Who They Leave Behind*. New York: Atria.

Bell, Derrick. 2018. *Faces at the Bottom of the Well: The Permanence of Racism*. Rev. ed. New York: Basic Books.

Berger, Michelle Tracey, and Kathleen Guidroz, eds. 2010. *The Intersectional Approach: Transforming the Academy through Race, Class, and Gender*. Chapel Hill: University of North Carolina Press.

Berry, Theodorea Regina, and Nathalie D. Mizelle. 2006. *From Oppression to Grace: Women of Color and Their Dilemmas in the Academy*. Sterling, Va.: Stylus.

Bessette, Lee Skallerup. 2014. "Creating Dialogue and Support for Undergraduate Women of Color." *Women in Higher Education* 23, no. 12: 1–2.

Blalock, Sacha D., and Rhonda Vonshay Sharpe. 2012. "You Go Girl! Trends in Educational Attainment of Black Women." In *Black American Female Undergraduates on Campus: Successes and Challenges*, edited by Rhonda V. Sharpe and Crystal Renee Chambers. Bingley, U.K.: Emerald Book Serials and Monographs.

Blee, Kathleen M. 1998. "White-Knuckle Research: Emotional Dynamics in Fieldwork with Racist Activists." *Qualitative Sociology* 21:381–99.

———. 2000. "White on White: Interviewing Women in U.S. White Supremacist Groups." In *Racing Research, Researching Race: Methodological Dilemmas in Critical Race Studies*, edited by France Winddance Twine and Jonathan W. Warren, 93–111. New York: New York University Press.

Bonilla-Silva, Eduardo. 2017. *Racism without Racists: Color-Blind Racism and the Persistence of Racial Inequality in America*. Lanham, Md.: Rowman and Littlefield.

Butler, Paul. 2013. "Black Male Exceptionalism? The Problems and Potential of Black Male–Focused Interventions." *Du Bois Review* 10:485–511.

Campbell, T. A., and D. E. Campbell. 2007. "Outcomes of Mentoring At-Risk College Students: Gender and Ethnic Matching Effects." *Mentoring & Tutoring: Partnership in Learning* 15, no. 2: 135.

Chambers, Crystal R., Rhonda V. Sharpe, and Henry Frierson, eds. 2012. *Black Female Undergraduates on Campus: Successes and Challenges*. Bingley, U.K.: Emerald.

Cole, Elizabeth. 2009 "Intersectionality and Research in Psychology." *American Psychologist* 64, no. 3: 170–80.

Coleman, M. Nicole, Stephanie Chapman, and David C. Wang. 2013. "An Examination of Color-Blind Racism and Race-Related Stress among African American Undergraduate Students." *Journal of Black Psychology* 39, no. 5: 486–504.

Collins, Patricia Hill. 1986. "Learning from the Outsider Within: The Sociological Significance of Black Feminist Thought." *Social Problems* 33, no. 6: 14–32.

———. 1999. "Moving beyond Gender: Intersectionality and Scientific Knowledge." In *Re-Visioning Gender*, edited by Myra Marx Ferree, Judith Lorber, and Beth B. Hess, 261–64. Thousand Oaks, Calif.: Sage.

———. 2000. *Black Feminist Thought: Knowledge, Consciousness, and the Politics of Empowerment*. 2nd ed. New York: Routledge.

———. 2004. *Black Sexual Politics: African Americans, Gender, and the New Racism*. New York: Routledge.

———. 2023. *Lethal Intersections: Race, Gender, and Violence*. New York: Polity.

Collins, Patricia Hill, and Sirma Bilge. 2016. *Intersectionality*. Cambridge, U.K.: Polity.

———. 2019. *Intersectionality*. 2nd ed. Cambridge, U.K.: Polity.

Combahee River Collective. 1983. "A Black Feminist Statement." In *This Bridge Called My Back: Writings by Radical Women of Color*, edited by Cherríe Moraga and Gloria Anzaldúa, 210–18. New York: Kitchen Table: Women of Color Press.

Connell, R. W. 2005. *Masculinities*. 2nd ed. Berkeley: University of California Press.

Covarrubias, Rebecca, and Stephanie A. Fryberg, S. A. 2015. "Movin' On Up (to College): First-Generation College Students' Experiences with Family Achievement Guilt." *Cultural Diversity and Ethnic Minority Psychology* 21, no. 3: 420–29.

Crawford, Vicki L. (1990) 2018. *Women in the Civil Rights Movement: Trailblazers and Torchbearers, 1941–1965*. Reprint. Bloomington: Indiana University Press.

Crenshaw, Kimberlé. 1989. "Demarginalizing the Intersection of Race and Sex: A Black Feminist Critique of Antidiscrimination Doctrine, Feminist Theory and Anti-Racist Politics." *University of Chicago Legal Forum* 1, no. 8: 139–67.

———. 1991. "Mapping the Margins: Intersectionality, Identity Politics, and Violence against Women of Color." *Stanford Law Review* 43, no. 6: 1241–99.

———. 1992. "Gender, Race, and the Politics of Supreme Court Appointments: The Import of the Anita Hill / Clarence Thomas Hearings: Race, Gender, and Sexual Harassment." *Southern California Law Review* 65:1467–76.

Dahlvig, Jolyn. 2010. "Mentoring of African American Students at a Predominantly White Institution (PWI)." *Christian Higher Education* 9, no. 5: 369–95.

Davis, Angela Y. 1981. *Women, Race & Class*. New York: Vintage.

Davis, Kathy. 2020. "Who Owns Intersectionality? Some Reflections on Feminist Debates on How Theories Travel." *European Journal of Women's Studies* 27, no. 2: 113–27.

Delgado, Richard, and Jean Stefancic. 2017. *Critical Race Theory: An Introduction*. 3rd ed. New York: New York University Press.

Eschmann, Rob. 2020. "Unmasking Racism: Students of Color and Expressions of Racism in Online Spaces." *Social Problems* 67:418–36.

Evans, Stephanie Y., Andrea D. Domingue, and Tania D. Mitchell, eds. 2019. *Black Women and Social Justice Education: Legacies and Lessons*. Albany: State University of New York Press.

Evans-Winters, Venus E., and Jennifer Esposito. 2010. "Other People's Daughters: Critical Race Feminism and Black Girls' Education." *Educational Foundations* 24, nos. 1–2: 11–24.

Evans-Winters, Venus E., and Bettina L. Love, eds. 2015. *Black Feminism in Education: Black Women Speak Back, Up, and Out*. New York: Peter Lang.

Foeman, Anita Kathy, and Bessie Lee Lawton. 2022. *Who Am I: Identity in the Age of Consumer DNA Testing*. San Diego: Cognella Academic.

Franklin, Jonathan. August 17, 2021. "Yik Yak, the Anonymous App That Tested Free Speech, Is Back." NPR. https://www.npr.org/2021/08/17/1028402237/yik-yak-anonymous-app-free-speech-returns.

Frye, Marilyn. 1983. *The Politics of Reality: Essays in Feminist Theory*. Trumansburg, N.Y.: Crossing Press.

Gaëtane, Jean-Marie, and Brenda Lloyd-Jones, eds. 2011. *Women of Color in Higher Education: Turbulent Past, Promising Future*. Bingley, U.K.: Emerald Group.

Guidroz, Kimberle, and M. T. Berger. 2010. "A Conversation with Founding Scholars of Intersectionality: Kimberlé Crenshaw, Nira Yuval-Davis, and Michelle Fine." In *The Intersectional Approach: Transforming the Academy through Race, Class, and Gender*, edited by M. T. Berger and K. Guidroz, 61–78. Chapel Hill: University of North Carolina Press.

Gutiérrez y Muhs, Gabriella, Yolanda Flores Niemann, Carmen G. González, and Angela P.

Harris, eds. 2012. *Presumed Incompetent: The Intersections of Race and Class for Women in Academia*. Logan: Utah State University Press.

Guy-Sheftall, Beverly, ed. 1995. *Words of Fire: An Anthology of African American Feminist Thought*. New York: New Press.

Hancock, Ange-Marie. 2007. "When Multiplication Doesn't Equal Quick Addition: Examining Intersectionality as a Research Paradigm." *Perspectives on Politics* 5, no. 1: 63–79.

Harding, Sandra. 2004. *The Feminist Standpoint Theory Reader: Intellectual and Political Controversies*. New York: Routledge.

Harris, Jessica C., and Lori D. Patton. 2019. "Un/Doing Intersectionality through Higher Education Research." *Journal of Higher Education* 90, no. 3: 347–72.

Hirshfield, Laura E., and Tiffany D. Joseph. 2012. "'We Need a Woman, We Need a Black Woman': Gender, Race, and Identity Taxation in the Academy." *Gender and Education* 24 no. 2: 213–27.

Hochschild, Arlie Russell. 1983. *The Managed Heart: Commercialization of Human Feeling*. Berkeley: University of California Press.

———. 2003. *The Commercialization of Intimate Life: Notes from Home and Work*. Berkeley: University of California Press.

hooks, bell. 1984. *Feminist Theory: From Margin to Center*. Boston: South End.

———. 1989. *Talking Back: Thinking Feminist, Thinking Black*. New York: Routledge.

———. 1992. *Black Looks: Race and Representation*. Boston: South End.

Iloh, Constance, and William Tierney. 2014. "Using Ethnography to Understand Twenty-First Century College Life." *Human Affairs* 24, no. 1: 20–39.

Jhally, Sut, producer and director. 1997. *Bell Hooks: Cultural Criticism & Transformation*. Northampton, Mass.: Media Education Foundation.

Jones, Mary E. 2015. "Intersectionality: Rejection or Critical Dialogue?" *Economic and Political Weekly* 50, no. 33: 72–76.

Jordan-Zachery, Julia. 2009. *Black Women, Cultural Images, and Social Policy*. New York: Routledge.

Kelly, Bridget Turner, Paige J. Gardner, Joakina Stone, Ashley Hixson, and Di-Tu Dissassa. 2019. "Hidden in Plain Sight: Uncovering the Emotional Labor of Black Women Students at Historically White Colleges and Universities." *Journal of Diversity in Higher Education* 14, no. 2: 203–16.

Kendall, Mikki. 2020. *Hood Feminism: Notes from the Women That a Movement Forgot*. New York: Viking.

King, Tiffany Lethabo. 2015. "Post-Indentitarian and Post-Intersectional Anxiety in the Neoliberal Corporate University." *Feminist Formations* 27, no. 3: 114–38.

Lenzy, Cherjanet D. 2019. "Navigating the Complexities of Race-Based Activism." In *Black Women and Social Justice Education: Legacies and Lessons*, edited by Stephanie Y. Evans, Andrea D. Dominigue, and Tania D. Mitchell, 261–74. Albany: State University of New York Press.

Lorde, Audre. 1984. *Sister Outsider*. Freedom, Calif.: Crossing.

Lubiano, Wahneema. 1998. *The House That Race Built: Original Essays by Toni Morrison,*

Angela Y. Davis, Cornel West, and Others on Black Americans and Politics in America Today. New York: Vintage Books.

Lugones, Maria C. 1987. "Playfulness, 'World'-Travelling, and Loving Perception." *Hypatia* 2, no. 2: 3–19.

———. 2006. "On Complex Communication." *Hypatia* 21, no. 3: 75–85.

Lugones, Maria C., and Elizabeth V. Spelman. 1983. "Have We Got a Theory for You! Feminist Theory, Cultural Imperialism, and the Demand for the 'Woman's Voice.'" *Women's Studies International Forum* 6, no. 6: 573–81.

Matti, Dominique. April 4, 2016. "Black Boys Need Two Talks." *Philadelphia Printworks* (blog). https://philadelphiaprintworks.com/blogs/zine/115117893-black-boys-need -two-talks.

McCall, Leslie. 2005. "The Complexity of Intersectionality." *Signs: Journal of Women in Culture and Society* 30:1771–800.

McIntosh, Peggy. 1988. "White Privilege and Male Privilege: A Personal Account of Coming to See Correspondences through Work in Women's Studies." Wellesley, Mass.: Wellesley College, Center for Research on Women.

Mills, Charles. 1997. *The Racial Contract.* Ithaca, N.Y.: Cornell University Press.

Mohanty, Chandra Talpade. 2003. *Feminism without Borders: Decolonizing Theory, Practicing Solidarity.* Durham, N.C.: Duke University Press.

———. 2013. "Transnational Feminist Crossings: On Neoliberalism and Radical Critique." *Signs: Journal of Women in Culture and Society* 38, no. 4: 967–91.

Moraga, Cherríe, and Gloria Anzaldua, eds. 1983. *This Bridge Called My Back: Writings by Radical Women of Color.* New York: Kitchen Table: Women of Color Press.

Musser, Amber Jamilla. 2015. "Specimen Days: Diversity, Labor, and the University." *Feminist Formations* 27, no. 3: 1–20.

Nash, Jennifer C. 2008. "Re-thinking Intersectionality." *Feminist Review* 89:1–16.

———. 2013. "Practicing Love: Black Feminism, Love-Politics, and Post-Intersectionality." *Meridians: Feminism, Race, Transnationalism* 11, no. 2: 1–24.

———. 2018. *Black Feminism Reimagined: After Intersectionality.* Durham, N.C.: Duke University Press.

Pascoe, C. J. 2007. *Dude, You're a Fag: Masculinity and Sexuality in High School.* Berkeley: University of California Press.

Puwar, Nirmal. 2004. *Space Invaders: Race, Gender, and Bodies out of Place.* New York: Berg.

Rodrigo, Richard. 1995. *The Rodrigo Chronicles: Conversations about Race in America.* New York: New York University Press.

Rodriguez, Dalia. 2011. "Silent Rage and the Politics of Resistance: Countering Seductions of Whiteness and the Road to Politicization and Empowerment." *Qualitative Inquiry* 17, no. 7: 589–98.

Rodriguez, Dalia, and Afua Boahene. 2012. "The Politics of Rage: Empowering Women of Color in the Academy." *Cultural Studies ↔ Critical Methodologies* 12, no. 5: 450–58.

Ross, Loretta. 2019. "Speaking Up without Tearing Down." *Teaching Tolerance Magazine* 61 (Spring).

Rothenberg, Paula S. 2002. *White Privilege: Essential Readings on the Other Side of Racism.* New York: Worth.

Ruchti, Lisa C. 2012. *Catheters, Slurs, and Pickup Lines: Professional Intimacy in Hospital Nursing.* Philadelphia: Temple University Press.

Sandoval-Lucero, Elena, Johanna B. Maes, and Libby Klingsmith. 2014. "African American and Latina(o) Community College Students' Social Capital and Student Success." *College Student Journal* 48, no. 3: 522–33.

Shavers, Marjorie C., and James L. Moore III. 2014. "The Double-Edged Sword: Coping and Resiliency Strategies of African American Women Enrolled in Doctoral Programs at Predominantly White Institutions." *Frontiers* 35, no. 3: 15–38, 209–10.

Smith, Barbara. 1983. *Home Girls: A Black Feminist Anthology.* Latham, N.Y.: Kitchen Table: Women of Color Press.

———. 1989. "A Press of Our Own: Kitchen Table: Women of Color Press." *Frontiers,* 10, no. 3: 11–13.

Smith, Buffy. 2015. *Mentoring At-Risk Students through the Hidden Curriculum of Higher Education.* New York: Lexington.

Smith, Dorothy. 1990. *The Conceptual Practices of Power: A Feminist Sociology of Knowledge.* Boston: Northeastern University Press.

———. 2005. *Institutional Ethnography: A Sociology for People.* Lanham, Md.: Alta Mira.

Smith, Michelle D., and Maia Niguel Moore. 2019. "Black Feminist Thought: A Response to White Fragility." In *Black Women and Social Justice Education: Legacies and Lessons,* edited by Stephanie Y. Evans, Andrea D. Domingue, and Tania D. Mitchell, 75–89. Albany: State University of New York Press.

Solorzano, Daniel, Miguel Ceja, and Tara Yosso. 2000. "Critical Race Theory, Racial Microaggressions, and Campus Racial Climate: The Experiences of African American College Students." *Journal of Negro Education* 69, nos. 1–2: 60–73.

Tatum, Beverly Daniel. 2008. *Can We Talk About Race? And Other Conversations in an Era of School Resegregation.* Boston: Beacon Press.

Twine, France Winddance, and Jonathan W. Warren, eds. 2000. *Racing Research, Researching Race: Methodological Dilemmas in Critical Race Studies.* New York: New York University Press.

Twine, France Winddance. 2000. "Racial Ideologies and Racial Methodologies." In *Racing Research, Researching Race: Methodological Dilemmas in Critical Race Studies,* edited by France Winddance Twine and Jonathan W. Warren, 1–34. New York: New York University Press.

Valentine, Gill. 2007. "Theorizing and Researching Intersectionality: A Challenge for Feminist Geography." *Professional Geographer* 59:10–21.

Warren, Jonathan W. 2000. "Masters in the Field: White Talk, White Privilege, White Biases." In *Racing Research, Researching Race: Methodological Dilemmas in Critical Race Studies,* edited by France Winddance Twine and Jonathan W. Warren, 135–64. New York: New York University Press.

Williams, Patricia. 1992. *The Alchemy of Race and Rights: Diary of a Law Professor.* Cambridge, Mass.: Harvard University Press.

Yenika-Agbaw, Vivian, and Amarilis Hidalgo de Jesus, eds. 2011. *Race, Women of Color, and the State University System: Critical Reflections*. Lanham, Md.: University Press of America.

Yuval-Davis, Nira. 2006. "Intersectionality and Feminist Politics." *European Journal of Women's Studies* 13, no. 3: 193–209.

Zelizer, Viviana A. 2005. *The Purchase of Intimacy*. Princeton, N.J.: Princeton University Press.

Zinn, Maxine Baca. 1979. "Field Research in Minority Communities: Ethical, Methodological, and Political Observations by an Insider." *Social Problems* 27:209–29.

Zinn, Maxine Baca, Lynn Weber Cannon, Elizabeth Higginbotham, and Bonnie Thorton Dill. 1990. "The Costs of Exclusionary Practices in Women's Studies." In *Making Face, Making Soul: Creative and Critical Perspectives by Women of Color*, edited by Gloria Anzaldúa, 29–41. San Francisco: Aunt Lute Books.

INDEX

academic exclusion, 57–58

Ahmed, Sara, 8, 27, 31–32, 43, 130

Allie (research participant), 37, 64–65, 113, 132

Anderson, Elijah, 25, 52, 81

anger and role expectations, 60

Anzaldúa, Gloria, 50, 60

Ari (research participant): on bridging labor, 61–62; on campus diversity claims, 21–22; on community knowledge, 107–8; on harassment, 95; on personal space violations, 89; on safe zones, 117, 138; on self-love, 115; on student government, 40–41, 133; on "the dance," 84; on tokenization, 55–56

Ava (research participant), 93

beauty standards, 90, 94–95, 112

"being the change," 116, 120–22

"being woke," 109–10

binary framing of identity, 80–81, 87

Black feminist epistemologies, 6–7, 105–6, 122. *See also* research methodology; women of color feminism

Black Feminist Thought (Collins), 105–6

"Black girl from Philly" (controlling image), 82–84, 101

Black Lives Matter protests, 51, 55, 61, 62, 69

Black male exceptionalism, 68–69

"Black mammy" (controlling image), 52–53

Black men and campus involvement, 65–70, 95

Black Student Union (NMU), 40, 67, 139

Blee, Kathleen, 149

boundaries and self-love, 113–15, 122

bridging labor: campus involvement/leadership and, 61–63, 66; classroom expectations and, 47–48, 55, 59; concept of, 48–49, 71–72; controlling images and, 52–53, 70–71; cultural taxation and, 54; as emotional labor, 7, 53; the fighter role and, 51–52, 56, 57–58; gender disparities and, 65–70; go-to role and, 51, 52, 55–56, 59; Greek life and, 63–65, 132–33; hypervisibility and invisibility of, 53–57; "intersectional invisibility" and, 67–68; multicultural organizations and, 133–34; performative behavior and, 59–60; sporting men of color and, 65–66; *This Bridge Called My Back* and, 49–51; tokenizing and, 55–57, 59. *See also* dilemma of diversity work

Brown, Michael, 66, 96

Butler, Paul, 68

"call in" learning process, 135

campus housing, 36–37

campus involvement, 39–42, 53, 61–63, 65–68

Carol (research participant), 22, 79–80, 96–97

Carolyn (research participant), 35, 39–40, 78, 91–92

cascading mentorship model, 137. *See also* mentorship

Cindy (research participant), 110, 115, 116

civil rights movement, 67

class, 37, 74, 80–81. *See also* "Black girl from Philly" (controlling image); "iconic ghetto" (controlling image); white, masculine, elite/middle-class spaces